Friends

Stories by Teenagers 2

**Edited by
Carl Koch**

**Saint Mary's Press
Christian Brothers Publications
Winona, Minnesota**

Genuine recycled paper with 10% post-consumer waste.
Printed with soy-based ink.

Amy Westerman, cover artist, Holy Cross High School, Louisville, KY

The publishing team included Carl Koch, development editor; Laurie A.
Berg, manuscript editor; Amy Schlumpf Manion, typesetter; Maurine R.
Twait, art director; pre-press, printing, and binding by the graphics
division of Saint Mary's Press.

Printed in the United States of America

Printing: 9 8 7 6 5 4 3 2 1

Year: 2005 04 03 02 01 00 99 98 97

ISBN 0-88489-492-4

Friends

...stop and consider
God's wonders.

Job 37:14

Dla Ani - rodzice

Lisa Wojtowicz
Pope John XXIII High School
Sparta, New Jersey

Contents

Preface

"Once upon a time . . ."

"Did you hear about the time . . . ?"

These phrases immediately attract our attention because human beings love listening to and telling stories. Storytelling is as natural as breathing, and as ancient as the cave dwellers' bragging and miming about the kill of the day around a campfire. We tell stories about the most serious events in our life, and the most wacky. We love stories for a lot of reasons:

Stories tell us who we are. When we tell other people a story, we reveal a lot about who we are—not only to them, but to ourselves. The poet Robert Frost says this about writing, "For me the initial delight is in the surprise of remembering something I didn't know I knew." In the hurry of life, we may have missed the importance of an event when it happened. Telling the story of the event helps us realize what the event really meant—even years later. So when we tell our story, we discover ourselves in new ways.

Stories help us feel less alone. As we listen to and tell stories, we realize that our story is a part of the great human story, that our feelings and experiences—while new and significant to us—are part of the universal human experience. We are not alone. Other people have felt as we do. Our story can affirm other people; their story can help us understand life better.

We encounter God in our stories. Many times when we tell stories, we begin to realize that life is filled with mystery. What we expect to happen does not happen; what does happen is unexpected. And frequently we begin to recognize the mysterious ways God has acted in our life.

We also listen to stories because they provide entertainment, because they are an outlet for our feelings and desires, and because they can make a point in an interesting way.

Stories by Teenagers

Teenagers enjoy telling their stories as much as anyone. Unfortunately, young women and men have few avenues for sharing their experiences and insights.

Saint Mary's Press has dedicated itself to sharing the Good News with young people. In the process, young people have shared their insights, courage, generosity, kindness, wisdom, patience, justice, and honesty—the Good News—with us.

Given our experience with two books of prayers and reflections by teenagers, *Dreams Alive* and *More Dreams Alive,* Saint Mary's Press decided to invite teenagers to share their stories. In October 1994, we asked the religion and English department chairpersons of all the Catholic high schools in the United States to invite their students to send their stories to us. The topic for the first volume of stories was teenagers' "most memorable experience of good coming out of a bad situation, or kindness in the midst of ugliness, or hope in darkness, or growth in the midst of difficulty."

Students could withhold their name, or use their initials, their first name, or their full name. We wanted to ensure that students could be honest in telling their stories. By April 1995, scores of stories had been submitted by high schools from coast to coast, Guam, and the U.S. Virgin Islands.

Six students and I selected the final forty-six stories for *I Know Things Now: Stories by Teenagers 1.* This first volume, published in May 1996, has been enthusiastically received by teenagers, parents, teachers, and all others who work with young men and women.

Friends: Stories by Teenagers 2

Given the encouraging response to the first book of stories by teenagers, we decided to publish a second volume. This time we asked teenagers in the United States, Canada, Ireland, England, and Australia to write stories about friends.

We chose the topic of friendship because our friends play such a vital role in our life. As the Scriptures say:

Faithful friends are a sturdy shelter:
  whoever finds one has found a treasure. . . .
Friends are life-saving medicine.

(Ecclesiasticus 6:14–16)

The wonderful stories illuminate this biblical wisdom.

Stories poured in from all over. After an initial sorting, I asked six students to help make the final selection: Rachel Dahdal, from Winona Senior High School; Tim Farrell, from Cotter High School; and Lushena Cook, John Corcoran, Hoa Dinh, and Denise Klinkner, from Saint Mary's University, all located in Winona, Minnesota. After studying hundreds of stories, we selected the forty-five in this book.

Thanks

Great thanks is due to all the students who allowed their stories to be submitted for consideration. The only unpleasant aspect of editing this book was having to omit so many excellent stories. They just could not all go into the book. We thank all of you for your contributions and understanding.

Thanks also go to the religion and English teachers who sent in the scores of stories received. Your cooperation made the book possible.

The stories contained here are fascinating and moving. They make inspiring personal reading, will serve as excellent discussion or reflection starters, and will find a welcome spot as readings for prayer services. They might even stimulate someone to write his or her own story. Each story shows how young people cherish, understand, remain loyal in, and build friendships. We hope that all who read these stories find inspiration, great hope, and renewed gratitude for friends.

Heather Barney
Oak Knoll School of the
Holy Child
Summit, New Jersey

The Fort

The dog days of August slowly come to a close, ushering in the worst week of the year: those torturous days between Labor Day weekend and the first day of a new school year. The pool is closed for the winter, likewise the tennis courts and any other possible form of summer recreation. The public schools have already opened, so I am stuck at home by myself with time to kill. It is no longer possible to escape the scorching summer heat since the air conditioner broke seventeen days ago (and counting) and has yet to be serviced. So I sit in my sweat-soaked clothes, chugging ice-cold lemonade and trying hard not to breathe—it would only create more hot air.

I have already completely exhausted the entire supply of even minutely interesting books the library has to offer, so I turn on the TV and find myself watching Oprah discuss women who say obese men make better lovers. Despite the fact that it is the third rerun of an episode I have already seen twice this month, I watch with mild interest until 537-pound Jerry stands up and starts a conga line through the studio audience with Matt (613 lbs.), Chuck (498 lbs.), and Barry (554 lbs.). Bored with even this fabulous display of talent, I head for the refrigerator where I meet up immediately with a bowl of jello that jiggles in a grotesque imitation of Barry's rear end. Maybe I'm not as hungry as I thought I was.

All other venues eliminated, I turn to the old standby: bothering my mother. After half an hour of humoring me and trying to think of some form of entertainment for me, she finally loses her temper. "Go for a walk in the woods with the dog," she cries as her last resort. So I do.

Clipping a leash onto his leather collar, I step out the door with my six-month-old golden retriever, Cisco, in tow, and we head up Chatham Street along the same route I had once taken as fast as my seven-year-old feet would take me. Here on the left is my old best friend Charlie's house, or at least it used to be. Yet another "For Sale" sign adorns the front lawn, the fifth that has been put up since Charlie moved away eight years ago. On the right is the McAdoo's old house. Mrs. McAdoo, one of my mother's best friends, was the first person I had ever known to pass away. She died of leukemia several years ago, leaving her three children motherless. Finally, past the torn and fading signs that once said "No Dumping," I can see the woods.

We jump the fence and hop down the low bank onto a deep bed of maple leaves. The smell of fresh dirt, rotting leaves, and wild animals rushes at me. I say wild animals, but don't get the wrong idea. The wildest thing we've ever had on Chatham Street was a raccoon that the police had to shoot right on our front lawn because they thought it might be rabid. Cisco's nose is already glued to the ground as he attempts to track a squirrel. Today I am in no rush, so I allow him to lead me off track a bit, but there was a time when I would run through these woods like a bullet intent upon my target. It is just now coming into sight, and I am amazed at how tiny it is compared to the picture I have carried in my mind for so long.

I'm guessing it's been close to seven years since I've been here, although I can't really remember how old I was when I stopped coming. The fort is still remarkably intact, considering that it's been half my lifetime since we laid down the final branch. I call it a fort, but it's really just three walls made out of sticks that have rotted away to practically nothing over the years. The packed dirt floor that we had once kept meticulously free of leaves is now buried under not only this year's leaves, but those of several years past. I pick up the rock that once marked the entrance to our castle, and watch as an inchworm and several pill bugs scurry for cover. Stepping inside, I clear away the leaves in one corner and sit down to rest for a few minutes. Even after tying Cisco's leash around a nearby tree, he continues searching for his squirrel.

Brett and I were just seven when we built the fort in the woods, which explains why the walls, just four feet high, had seemed so towering in my memory. The fort was neutral ground where neither of us had to play host or hostess and where we could be away from our older siblings and parents, if only for a little while. Its location, roughly equidistant between his house on Fairfax Terrace and mine on Chatham Street, was perfect because we could meet halfway and neither of us could complain of having the farther distance to walk. In addition, it was secluded enough to allow us the freedom to play as loudly as we liked, but still close enough to home that our mothers wouldn't worry too much about what we were up to.

We would stay for hours, playing He-Man and Thundercats and every other game a seven-year-old tomboy and her friend can imagine. Brett owned the complete Masters of the Universe set, including a two-foot-high Castle Greyskull, complete with a trapdoor, where Skeletor reigned supreme. On the other hand, I had just about every Star Wars figure ever made, from Chewbacca the Wookie to Darth Vader. However, the highlight of my collection was my Millennium Falcon model, which Brett could touch only under careful supervision.

But what I remember most about Brett doesn't have anything to do with our toys or with the fort. Brett introduced me to peanut butter and honey sandwiches and the honey bear. Honey bear was a plastic squeeze bottle with a red cap shaped like a bear. It held the Wilson's honey and was always standing ready on their kitchen table. I used to pester my mother constantly to get us one, and I think we did have one for a while, although I don't know what ever happened to it. It's been years since I've had a peanut butter and honey sandwich, but I can almost taste the gooey concoction and feel a sticky drop of honey as it oozes out the edges and crawls down my leg. I really don't think I ever saw Brett eat anything but those delicious creations, and I often wondered if that was his entire diet. No, that's not quite true. There is a picture in the scrapbook of Brett and me and our friend Megan sitting on a bench outside on a sunny day "eating" plastic bagels. And there was the time Brett and I picked, cleaned, and ate onion grass. We both stayed home from school the next day because we were very sick to our stomachs.

But things change with time. Brett began playing with boys because they could run faster or throw farther than I could. I found girls to play with, and in time I traded in my Star Wars figures for Barbie dolls and the like. Time passed, and we were suddenly thrown into the world of fifth grade with new faces and new unspoken social laws. In this new and strange world, girls and guys weren't allowed to be friends like before unless they were "going out." And that was far beyond Brett and me.

More time passed and more changes. We made new friends and burned more bridges. And suddenly one day, I found myself walking home from school with a complete stranger who looked like Brett and sounded like Brett but was not Brett. But still, in this stranger I find a new friend who is different from my old friend, and yet so much the same. We can no longer play and carry on with the honesty we once did, but perhaps in a way this new friendship is even more honest because we don't have to pretend to be He-Man and Skeletor; we can just be ourselves.

Cisco's relentless barking wakes me from my reverie, and I see that he has finally chased a squirrel up a tree, but is wondering where to proceed from there. It seems I drifted off for a while, because it is growing dark in the woods. I get up, wipe the dirt off my pants, and see something I had not noticed before. The moist ground has preserved perfectly a set of large footprints leading into and out of the fort, and off in the direction of Fairfax. They are perhaps as much as a day or two old and are beginning to disappear, but I know whose they are. Replacing the rock to where I found it, I untie Cisco and head back the way I came, leaving my own footprints in the mud. I have found what I came for.

J. T. A. G.
La Salle College High School
Wyndmoor, Pennsylvania

All You've Got

For me, the past New Year's Eve was one that I'll never forget: I almost lost the person who has been my best friend since kindergarten.

Jack and I met one day over the Tonka truck during playtime, two weeks into my first year of school. A big oaf of a five-year-old named Craig came over and told me to give the truck to him. At first, I was reluctant because it was the best toy they had and the chances of getting it again were slim. However, this being the first day in school for me, I felt that, as the new kid, I had to prove how nice and friendly I was. So I obliged, courteously handing it over to him.

Just as Craig was saying, "Thanks, wuss!" Jack came over and told Craig: "Give it back to the new kid, Craig. Don't make me hafta pound ya!"

Now, Jack wasn't nearly as big as this kid who had practically begun growing facial hair, but he could make a much meaner looking face. Jack put his worst frown on, bunched his eyes close together so it looked like he only had one eyebrow, and said in his best "dad voice," "Give it to him now!" Craig tried to look calm, but he ended up just looking confused, which was pretty normal for this kid. He reluctantly handed the truck back to me. Jack and I have been friends ever since.

This past New Year's Eve I had gotten stuck with working at the fancier of the two restaurants where I'd been working at

16

the time. I was dishwashing faster than ever before because I knew that Jack was having a little get–together at his house and, call me crazy, but I felt that I would have a better time there than at work. So I called him at about 11:00 p.m. to tell him that I might be dropping by after work if everyone was still awake.

Sean, a friend of ours from our old school, picked up the phone. I asked for Jack, and Sean told me that he was in the bathroom. I said I'd wait, but Sean informed me that it might be a while. Jack had been throwing up for the past half hour, and it didn't look like it was going to slow up any time soon. He said that Jack had had too much to drink and was in really bad shape.

I couldn't believe what I was hearing. Jack had never really drank before except for a few shots of liquor one time while I was over at his house. Other than that, he was the cleanest guy I knew. He didn't smoke pot, he didn't smoke cigarettes, he didn't dip. And now he was practically puking up a lung be-cause he had had too much to drink.

My boss was starting to yell at me to get back to work, so I had to go. Worried about Jack though, I told Sean that I'd be calling back. He said, "Fine," and abruptly hung up.

As I went back to dishing, my thoughts raced. I couldn't understand what could have happened. Jack didn't know anyone who could have gotten him beer, so I figured he must have been drinking liquor. Not good for a lightweight. That also explained why the other people there hadn't stopped him earlier. When you drink liquor, you can't keep track of yourself because it takes a while to get to you. So by the time he'd started feeling it, it must have already been too late for him to stop.

I called back at 11:55 to see how Jack was doing. This time Mark picked up the phone. I asked if Jack was all right, and whether or not I should come over when I was done with work.

"No," he replied, "I don't think that would be a good idea. The police are here and so are the paramedics. Jack's going to the hospital."

I was stunned. I couldn't move. Everything just seemed to slow down to a crawl. It wasn't really as if the moment was frozen in time, but more like slowed down enough so that I could comprehend the full gravity of the moment. My best friend, whom I had known for almost eleven years, was being put into an ambulance and taken to the hospital because he had had too much to drink. The idea was so alien to me that I had to have Mark repeat it twice before it finally sunk in. I asked if Jack's parents were there. They weren't. I told Mark to take care of Jack and hung up.

All that night I couldn't get to sleep. I kept thinking about what would happen if it turned out to be really bad, and Jack died. I began to envision life without him, but it hurt too much. I kept trying to rationalize by saying, "No one dies from one night of drinking too much. They just get really bad headaches." But the worst case scenario always popped back into my head.

The next morning I called Jack's private line and his house line—no answer at either. I left a message on his private line telling him to call me back as soon as possible. Then, at 10:30 a.m., he called. He sounded really weak. I looked up and thanked God, and then listened as he related his night to me.

He said that he didn't have his stomach pumped to his knowledge, but he was unconscious for the most part, so he didn't know for sure. He said his blood alcohol level had been .18. It was now down to .10, still legally drunk. He said that he really appreciated my calls last night and this morning, and that he had to go because he needed his rest.

Before he hung up, I told him that I was really worried and that he shouldn't try so hard to have fun next time. He told me he wouldn't and hung up. I know that this sounds like a really mushy thing to say, but when you spend practically all of your time with a certain person or group of people, you can't help but to start to care about them, I don't care who you are. Sometimes you don't even realize that it's happening, but you develop feelings for them. You start to get used to them being around. And when they stop being around, that's when you realize you need these people, because really, they're all you've got.

Nate Scatena
University of San Diego High School
San Diego, California

Kathy Grasso
Saint Maria Goretti
High School
Philadelphia, Pennsylvania

Presents

Two years ago, I learned that the word *Christmas* does not mean the giving or receiving of presents, the smell of fresh trees, or turkeys roasting in the oven. No, the true meaning of Christmas is friendship.

My story is a simple one. It tells of two best friends, myself and Jenny, who come to realize that the meaning of Christmas cannot be purchased in stores or found on the inside of a card. It is found, rather, in the one place where many people seldom look—their heart.

"What do you want for Christmas?" I asked Jenny as we walked home from school one cold December afternoon.

"I don't know. I haven't really given it much thought," Jenny replied with a shrug.

"How can you not give it much thought?! I can't stop thinking about it!" I said excitedly.

"Well, what do you want for Christmas?" Jenny asked with a smile and a shake of her head.

"I don't know. I haven't really given it much thought," I replied with a grin. A minute passed before we both laughed hysterically.

"C'mon. It's freezing out here," Jenny complained as we stood on my front step.

"I'm hurrying, I'm hurrying," I said as my almost numb hands fumbled with the keys.

"Jen, we're friends right?" I asked, somewhat unsure if I should continue.

"Of course we are," Jenny replied with a puzzled look on her face. "Why?"

"Well, I don't think this is going to be a very good Christmas for my family. We don't have a lot of money this year, and I'm afraid I might not be able to get you anything for Christmas," I explained, waiting nervously for her reaction.

"Kathy, you know we're best friends, and I'll understand if you don't get me anything for Christmas."

"You, you will?"

"Of course! That's what makes me your best friend. My wonderful ability to understand," Jenny said, trying to keep a straight face.

"Oh! But of course," I replied in return. Both of us managed to keep straight faces for only a few seconds. When we could not hold out any longer, we burst out laughing.

Jenny came over Christmas morning to give me my gift. As I opened it, I felt embarrassed about giving Jenny her's. I was surprised to see that she bought me a Snoopy watch.

"Thank you!" I said.

"Oh, you're welcome."

It was my turn to give Jenny her gift. "It's not much, Jen." The rectangular box with red wrapping paper and a green bow held a single piece of paper inside. It read:

Dear Jenny,
I know you were expecting to get a really nice gift this year. I told you I could not afford to get the ring you wanted or your favorite perfume. Instead, the gift is one that cannot be purchased in stores or found on the inside of a card. It is the one gift that is and always will be well appreciated. That gift is friendship. Merry Christmas!
Your friend, Kathy

Jenny looked up with a tear in her eye. A minute of silence passed.

"Thank you," Jenny replied. "It's the best gift I've ever received! Merry Christmas, Kathy!"

"Merry Christmas, Jen. Merry Christmas."

Samantha Ecker
Saint Joseph Hill Academy
Staten Island, New York

Annie's Gift

When I was ten years old, I had a lot of friends. But looking back now, my best friend was someone I never really thought of as my friend. I only considered Annie my next-door neighbor.

I didn't know too much about Annie. She was four years older than I was. She went to an art school in the city. Every afternoon as I played in the front yard with my little brother Kevin, I would see Annie walking home from the train station. I remember admiring how mature she looked carrying her big black portfolio as her pretty blonde hair blew in the wind. I'd see her bright, friendly smile, and I'd run up to her to say hello. I admired the freckles that graced her face. Annie was the only person I knew who had freckles. I wished that I had freckles and that I was old enough to go to school with her.

Sometimes on weekends, Annie would make up games for Kevin and me to play. We'd go on treasure hunts and put on plays about stories that Annie told to us. Her stories kept us fascinated for hours. I admired a lot of things about Annie, but what I admired most was her imagination.

When Kevin and I would get into trouble and be sent to our rooms, we would look across the driveway to Annie's house. We'd look in the window to see if she was there. If she was, we had a Morse code system devised by Annie to send secret messages to each other.

Once Annie showed us the mural she painted on her bedroom wall. In every color you could imagine, she had painted an assortment of cartoon characters. In my mind, Michelangelo could not have done a more impressive job.

During the summer there was always something to do, thanks to Annie. She would teach us art techniques and show us how to make stone people. She'd make up intricate plots with interesting characters for us to portray. By September, Kevin and I had been spies, detectives, and a myriad of other characters.

One day I was sitting outside on the porch. It was my birthday, but I was sad. I can't remember why. Annie appeared out of nowhere and presented me with a birthday card and a drawing she had done of me. To this day, I still don't know how Annie remembered my birthday, but I'm glad she did.

Now I'm seventeen. Annie is twenty-one. I only see her warm, friendly smile once in a while, but it's the same smile she used to flash at me seven years ago. I'm in high school now, and when I get home from the train station, I see Alex, the little boy who lives down the street, watching me. When I smile at him, he runs up and asks me if I want to play. Sometimes I make up games for Alex and his sister Jenny. Sometimes I think of treasure hunts for them to go on. I teach them the art techniques that Annie taught me. I watch Alex and Jenny laugh as they play with their stone people. It reminds me of when I was ten and when one of the most important people in my life was someone who I never even realized was my best friend.

Erica Balhoff
Saint Joseph's Academy
Baton Rouge, Louisiana

Words of Encouragement

The relationship shared by my sister and me is similar to any normal sister relationship. We have had our childhood fights over clothes, household rules, and many other ridiculous conflicts. She never failed to call me her shadow when I wanted to be with her because, naturally, she was agitated at my being the epitome of a tagalong.

Although I was a nuisance to her as a child, we grew out of the little sister-big sister phase, and we became best friends. As the years passed, my sister and I became partners in dancing, and those who watched us remarked about how much we resembled one another in the style of our dance and our appearance on stage. As the little sister, I was so proud to be told that I was the exact image of my older sister because I had looked up to her for as long as I could remember.

She had always watched me perform when she was not able to dance herself. Her encouragement and advice pushed me to be my best on stage. I never failed to meet her standards, for I wanted not only to win for myself, but also to impress her and make her proud of me.

I can remember back to a time when I was at summer dance camp for the week. I should have been enjoying the time with my friends, but my enjoyment was tempered by the absence of my sister. She was called out of town and was not able to see me perform with my team. Loneliness and misery surrounded me that week, but somehow I pulled through the emptiness when the last day of competition came. I had practiced for hours.

Somehow my dad managed to find me among the hundreds of dancers in the enormous auditorium. To my amazement, he handed me a brown paper bag colorfully decorated and filled with an assortment of candy. At the bottom, I came across a card with a picture of two small girls, greatly resembling my sister and me, standing in the rain, sharing an umbrella. As I proceeded to open the card, I found a letter written by my sister:

> Dear Sis,
>
> Sorry I couldn't come see you dance tonight, but I know you will do great. During the past year I have watched you develop into a very talented dancer. Always hold your head high and keep smiling, and I am positive you will be the best. I'll see you later. Have a good time at camp.
>
> Love always,
> Me

As I drank in her words, tears flooded my eyes. Emotion completely enveloped me. The next minute I was sobbing. I could hardly breathe. I was so overwhelmed by her confidence in me because I had always strived to be just like her. Suddenly the physical absence of my sister was replaced with her spirit. Her pride in me made me feel proud, not only of my ability to dance but also of the person I had become, a person like her.

Ever since that letter, my sister and I have only become better friends. We are there for each other at any time of need, just as her presence was there for me when I felt lonely and abandoned that day. Whenever I need reassurance from someone or something, I take out those soothing words of encouragement that I saved and read them for solace because I treasure them as the greatest gift I have ever received.

Timothy A. Kearney
Immaculate High School
Danbury, Connecticut

Sign My Book

When I was seven years old, I moved from Mission Viejo, California, to Norco, California. I had to change schools, which meant making new friends.

On the first day at Saint Mel's School, my second-grade teacher, Mrs. Duperron, gave us little heart-shaped books. She instructed us to go around the room and have people whom we wanted to get to know better sign our books. All of a sudden I heard a voice ask, "Would you sign my book?" When I looked up, I saw an unimaginably tall second grader. His name was Todd.

Todd Ramasar was born in New York City on August 24, 1979. Right after he was born, Todd and his family moved to California. His mother, Ghislaine, was from Haiti, and his father, Oskar, was from French Guiana. Todd has an older brother named Kirk, also born in New York City. After moving to California, Oskar worked for the telephone company and "Gigi" was a nurse. However, they later started their own business, owning and operating a nursing home.

Eventually, Todd and I started hanging out together. We got to be great friends, mainly through our brothers who were the same age and also good friends. My mother was also Kirk's teacher for two years in a row. Todd and I did everything together. We would visit each other's home, and play basketball, football, and other sports together.

One day I went over to Todd's house. When my mother came to pick me up, Mrs. Ramasar invited her in to chat for a while. They hit it off perfectly and became the best of friends. In fact, soon both sets of our parents became great friends. Now that our parents were friends, Todd and I became almost inseparable. Our families met at least once a week for pizza, and we spent some weekends together at the beach.

As the years went on, our friendship grew, and so did Todd. In sixth grade, Saint Mel's School was having a lot of problems. The school went through six teachers, and was forced to close due to financial difficulties. For a while we were afraid that we would end up at different schools. Our parents did everything in their power to put us in the same school, Our Lady of Perpetual Help in Riverside.

Since we both didn't know very many people at our new school, we stuck together most of the time until we became better acquainted with others. Before we knew it, we were graduating from the eighth grade and were off to high school. We both decided to attend Notre Dame High School in Riverside, which was the same high school that our brothers attended. Todd had received many offers to attend other high schools because of his extraordinary basketball talents.

In our freshman year, Todd blossomed as a basketball star. As a freshman, he was a starter on the varsity team and one of the leading scorers. As Todd's talents grew, so did his popularity. Everyone wanted to be Todd Ramasar's friend. Recruiting letters came in weekly, and I was afraid that Todd would forget about me and the rest of our mutual friends. He didn't. In fact, he still chose to spend his free time with me, and his popularity never went to his head.

At the beginning of our sophomore year, Todd decided to attend the public school near his home because of their strong basketball program. Once again I was worried that Todd would make new friends and forget about his old ones. I was wrong again. Although we didn't see each other at school every day, we still did lots of things together on the weekends. Sometimes I was even able to attend the basketball games at his new school.

As fate would have it, I moved from California to Connecticut in the middle of my sophomore year. Since I've moved here, we still keep in touch and so do our parents. Although we live far away from each other, we still consider ourselves best friends. I know that he will come and visit me in Connecticut, and I have already been out to visit him in California. In fact, I expect that we will remain lifelong friends.

Stacy Williams
Saint Agnes Academy
Memphis, Tennessee

L. S.
Mount Saint Joseph Academy
Flourtown, Pennsylvania

Everlasting

As I brought the car to a complete stop, I shifted into park and turned off the engine. My friends Ashley and Courtney were waiting outside the car while I grabbed the bouquet of flowers that I had left on the seat.

"It's a good thing the grass is starting to grow back. Otherwise, we'd have to sit on the dirt," Ashley observed as we walked past a line of tombstones.

The sky was a deep blue with not a cloud in sight, and the warm sun shone through the branches of the trees. There was complete silence except for the occasional rustling of the wind through the trees.

"Hello, Doug," I said as we sat down on a patch of newly planted grass.

"I wonder when he's going to get a tombstone," Courtney inquired.

"It's only been four months," Ashley answered as she spread out the flowers we had brought. "They have to wait for the ground to settle."

"It doesn't seem like it's been four months already. I feel like he was alive yesterday. Doesn't it seem like we just went out with him? Remember that time we went bowling, and he kept going on everyone else's turn so that the scores got all mixed up."

"Yeah, he got strikes when he bowled for Robin, but he always shot gutterballs when it counted for his turn," I offered. "How about the time I caught him with my camera, taking all those pictures of people's feet. The things that amused him were amazing. My parents still give me a lecture on wasting film."

"Yeah, and Doug," Ashley said, "remember that time in eighth grade when we stood up to say prayers and you pulled my chair out from underneath me. I fell flat on the ground, and we both just couldn't stop laughing."

As we recited all the wonderful memories we shared with Doug, I had almost forgotten that he had died of cancer that spring. Then, I looked down at my hand and remembered the quote from the funeral mass booklet: "I will never forget you, Doug. I have carved you in the palm of my hand." I also remembered my body feeling numb as I stumbled through the church doors that morning. I could not erase from my mind the image I had seen the previous evening of that stranger's body lying in the casket. That figure was not the Doug that I knew. My friend Doug always wore a smile and made people laugh.

During the Mass, Doug's aunt gave a beautiful eulogy. "I admired Doug," she said, "because I never once heard him complain of the pain he was going through. In fact, he seemed to live the normal life of a fifteen-year-old boy. He kept good grades and went to sixteenth birthday parties and, just last month, a high school formal."

These words had been true, but I was shocked to hear her next words.

"That Thursday night before he died," she said, "Doug held my hand tightly and whispered, 'I'm ready to go.'"

Through my tear-filled eyes, I could see some of my best friends crying. I wanted to hug them, but the church pews separated us.

As I reached into my pocket for another tissue, Doug's neighbor rose and said, "Doug was the kind of kid that was popular for all the right reasons." This had been so true.

When the Mass ended, all of Doug's best friends rose to carry the casket. At first glance, I wondered who was missing. Usually all five of them were together, but today there were only four. As the four best friends grabbed the handles of the casket, it hit me. I could just imagine how hard it was for them to carry their best friend to his grave.

"Lauren, are you ready to go?" asked Ashley as she tapped me on the shoulder.

"Bye, Doug, we'll be back to visit you soon," said Courtney. "If you're lucky, maybe we'll bring you an Irish flag."

As we walked back to the car, I turned around and whispered: "I will never forget you, Doug. I have carved you in the palm of my hand."

Colleen J. Duffy
Saint Scholastica Academy
Chicago, Illinois

Mr. Pinter

Friendship can come in many different degrees and forms. It simply cannot be summed up in just one word. If one was to ask teenagers what a friend is, they probably would all answer in basically the same way. Similarly, if one was to ask a child, a middle-aged person, or a senior citizen, he or she would probably answer in a way close to how people his or her own age answered. So, one can say that a person's vision of friendship changes throughout a person's life. People of every age will agree that it would be incredibly hard, if not impossible, to go through life friendless. In fact, it is simply amazing to think about how many friends have weaved in and out of one's life. People usually only consider being friends with people their own age. In truth, there is no age restriction for friendship.

As I was growing up, I went to church every Sunday. At church I met Mr. Pinter. At that time he was probably in his early nineties. He was not what one might expect from someone that old, though. He was not hard of hearing or slow in any way. Instead, he was alert and kind.

I remember him giving me small presents when I was little, such as a card with a dollar in it. A dollar may seem like small change now, but to a child it is a huge sum of money. He was like a surrogate grandfather to me because I never knew either of my grandfathers. I was special to him, too, because I have the same name as one of his nieces.

Soon he moved to Wisconsin, but he occasionally visited with my family. On holidays he would send me greeting cards, which I cherished. Naturally I was delighted to receive something in the mail.

When he did visit, it was a treat to see him. He taught me that you are only as young as you feel, and that, while many people consider senior citizens to be lost in a time warp, our generation has a lot to learn from them. I also learned that it does not have to be a misfortune to grow old—but in many ways it can be a blessing.

I can remember him teaching me a game similar to games like tic-tac-toe or hangman. It had to do with initialing the most number of squares out of a series of dots. We had a lot of fun playing that game. I guess I must have been amazed because I probably thought that older people did not know of such games, or at least did not keep up with them.

He lived to the age of ninety-seven, dying, mostly, of old age. I was sad when I found out he had died because I knew I had lost a great friend. Although, seeing as he lived for ninety-seven good years, I was happy that he was going to finally be with God and be reunited with deceased friends and family. He taught me a lot of things for which I am grateful. He was a blessing to everybody who knew him, and a man who will hardly be forgotten.

Guy G. Werner III
Union Catholic Regional
High School
Scotch Plains, New Jersey

The Bible Incident

The back door to Universal needed, as always, a gentle nudge to open. The door was never put on straight enough, so it scraped along the bottom of the floor. Most comic book shops don't even have a back door, so I never complained. The month was March and still cold, so I shut the door tightly behind me and turned to see who was around.

My good friend Steve was behind the counter, as I knew he would be. He smiled when he saw me. It had been a slow day, so I was a welcome distraction.

"Guy-Dog!" Steve greeted me with the usual nickname.

"Steve-Dog!" I answered back in kind.

"How you doing?"

"The usual. How 'bout you?"

"Oh, man. Am I glad to see you. This place has been dead. I mean, like, no one has been in here. Drag city. It's been me and the CD player all morning. And you know what the boss man did this morning? He chewed me out today at freakin' seven o'clock, when farmers are still sleeping, about the garbage from two days ago. I swear I'm gonna kill 'em."

Steve had been having a lot of problems lately, so I understood when he started to complain right off the bat. I had come just to see how he was doing actually. His mother had just moved out of the house, he was stuck in a below minimum wage job, and college wasn't in the picture. At nineteen years of age, he was thinking about the future he didn't have and was pretty depressed about it.

I had just sat down when, of all people, his mother walked in the front door. Steve stood up and gave me a puzzled look. "Watch the store for me while I'm out, okay man?" I told him it was no problem. He walked outside with his mother and they lit cigarettes and began to talk. Both he and his mom were chain smokers. The apple doesn't fall far from the tree. Through the glass storefront, I could see them as they talked, and it didn't look like a happy conversation. They were clearly arguing, and it ended with his mother charging off down the street. Steve stormed back into the shop.

"My life is over! I should just end it now! My mom wants a divorce, and she's leaving us. She doesn't even care. It's like we just don't matter to her! What's my father going to do?"

All I could say was, "Man, I'm sorry."

Defeated, Steve sank into his chair behind the counter and stared blankly at the wall. I tried to comfort him, took a stab at small talk, and after a short time gave up. It was quiet in the store.

The front door opened.

"Steve?"

"Who's that?" Steve asked, without even looking. I had never seen the odd-looking guy who had just entered, but he looked around our age.

Once again, the stranger spoke: "Steve?"

"Uh, Adam?" Steve gave me a second look, more puzzled than the first, and asked me to watch the store again. I answered in the affirmative, and again Steve went to talk outside the glass storefront with a visitor. Adam handed Steve some sort of package and, after a brief exchange, he waved good-bye and made his way up the street.

Curious about what had just gone on, I was quick to ask Steve about who this new friend was and the purpose of his visit. "That was my friend Adam. I haven't seen him in years. We used to go to middle school together. He just said he was think-ing of me and had something he thought I should have."

With that, Steve put the mysterious package on a table and we examined it. It appeared to be a heavy box or book wrapped in newspaper. There was nothing of interest on the outside so Steve ripped it open to reveal a Bible.

A letter was folded into the first page. The first few lines read as follows:

Dear Steve,
I know we haven't seen each other in a while, but I've been thinking of you and know you are going through tough times. I figured you could use some help and I know of someone that can give it to you. I'm referring to God.

Kimberly A. Milford
Saint Agnes Academy
Memphis, Tennessee

More Than a Friend

As my thirteenth summer began, each day was filled with attending younger siblings' sporting events, catching up on my assigned summer reading, and occasionally sneaking in a little time with my friends. Despite a few complaints, the fact that there would be no school for three months had finally set in, and everything was really going well, until a break in the action made me realize how important our friends and loved ones really are.

The phone rang at about nine o'clock one night. Mom was getting ready for bed after an exhausting summer's day and, for some reason that I've forgotten, the entire family had gathered in my parents' bedroom. Mom answered the phone and, as she listened, I saw the color drain from her face, leaving it a pallid white. As I soon found out, a running mate and friend of my older brother had been in a serious car accident earlier that day and he was in critical condition at the Med. His friends and family were calling to ask for prayers.

Immediately, out came the rosary beads and, for the first time in a long while, we prayed together as a family. Between decades, we received updates on his condition, but before we were finished, the doctors were not expecting him to survive the night. By this time we were all upset, trying to fathom losing such a friend. I turned, and for the first time in my life, I saw my "big brother" *really* cry. The next morning, my brother's friend Peter was pronounced dead.

A few days later, a tearful memorial service was held. Because of the violent nature of the accident, Peter's family had his body cremated and his ashes spread over one of his favorite places: his team's running course. From then on, anyone who doubted his presence within the team was truly mistaken.

This year would have been his senior year in high school. He had been one of the best runners on the team, and if he were alive today, he still would be. Over the past two years, the team had worked hard and had qualified to compete in the state championship.

Before the officials fired the gun to begin the race, the team stepped aside, said a prayer, and remembered their late friend. Not only was God with them, but Peter was in each of their hearts.

The race began, and the team performed remarkably. Peter was definitely shining down on them from heaven. As one of the runners crossed the finish line, I heard him say as he looked up at the sky, "This one's for you, Pete!" Peter had made a greater impact on the team than anyone would have thought two years ago, and he had become more than a friend to them—he was an inspiration.

Jessica Marie Radwill
Oak Knoll School of the
Holy Child
Summit, New Jersey

You're It

Until I was five years old, my neighbor and best friend, Jason, came over daily so we could make up puppet shows in my basement, run races in the street, play tag in the yard, swing on my jungle gym, or have peanut butter and jelly sandwiches on my back porch. If I went to his house, we could race Big Wheels in his driveway, watch shows on his big-screen TV, snack on the endless supply of popsicles in his freezer, build tents beneath his bunk beds, or compete in tough board games such as Candy Land, Alphabet Soup, and Chutes and Ladders. No matter what activity occupied us, I always had an extraordinary time.

On my face was a permanent grin, and my pigtails swung like the wagging tail of a young golden retriever. Our days together, packed with exciting activities, seemed perpetual, and when the sun's last rays eventually disappeared behind the trees next to the McHugh's house across the street, I was so exhausted that I parted agreeably, satisfied with the knowledge that I would see my friend again in the morning.

These glorious days of carefree play came to a surprising halt in the fall when I began kindergarten at a private, Catholic school in another town. That September marked the first time in my lifetime of five years that I was separated from Jay for so many hours at a time. We continued to play after school until somewhere around November or early December, but soon the days got too cold to play outside and we saw very little of each other since he and I both made new friends at our schools.

The distance that formed between Jason and me upset me, but on February 14, 1984, he called my house and asked me to come over so he could show me something new. Expecting a neat BMX bike or another extravagant toy he could show off to me, I ran over to uncover his surprise.

He brought me out to his deck and we sat down on his hammock, each in the established spot that we had sat in a million times before. The oak tree overhead was bare, and I remembered all the times I had sneezed beneath the tree that made me so allergic. I was recalling the stuffy nose and itchy eyes I had endured, so he caught me off guard when he pulled out a small section of the Morris County Daily Journal and pointed to a message written in red ink on the Valentine's Day special page in the bottom corner. The note caught my eye immediately because I spied my name, Jessie, in bold print, and he told me what the rest said as I followed along with my developing reading skills: "Happy Valentine's Day to my pal. Love, Jason."

I grinned to see that he had remembered me. We rocked slowly toward the railing, then back near the oak tree. I smiled again and hit him hard on the shoulder. "You're it," I whispered, then scrambled down the steps into the snowy yard. We continued the game that had been cut short by my enrollment at Oak Knoll, and though I lost tag by forfeit when my mother called me in for dinner, I was triumphant in reviving a defunct friendship that I believed was as irreparable as the lifeless oak tree.

Scott Gosselin
Xaverian Brothers
High School
Westwood, Massachusetts

Being There

Friendship is a funny thing. If you turn your back on it you feel bad, but if you accept friends into your life they can make you feel, like, terrible. But friends come through for you and are there when you need them. If I had to talk about one friend who has made a huge difference in my life, it wouldn't be anyone that I have met at school. The person who has had the biggest impact on my life would have to be my dad.

It is kind of hard to imagine that a parent could be your best friend, but my dad is. Friends have come and gone, and to tell you the truth, I have never given them another thought. But my dad has always been there for me and has always tried to help me realize how special I am to him. All my life he has driven me from rink to rink, ball field to ball field, and has never griped. He not only drives me, but enjoys watching and occasionally participating.

I guess I realized how much my father's friendship meant to me a couple of years ago on a Saturday night. As usual, we had to go to a hockey arena in the middle of nowhere. This was a normal weekend occurrence. We would get into the car at eleven in the morning and usually not be home until around eight at night. We were in the car forever it seemed. But spending all that time together brought us closer and we got to know each other better.

We had driven about two hours and had finally arrived at the rink. Game time was at three in the afternoon, and at this point it was one o'clock. So we had plenty of time to get a bite to eat and then go to the game. When we got back to the rink though, we realized that the game was at a new rink an hour away. Needless to say, we flew out of the parking lot and headed south.

We finally got to the right rink only minutes before game time. I ran inside only to find that the game had been delayed by an hour because of a Zamboni malfunction. But the big problem was that the coach had not shown up. So my dad volunteered to lead the charge against the Merrimack Valley Cardinals. We ended up winning the game and going home happy.

Of course, all the discussion on the way home was the game and how I played. I think that I never play well in his opinion, but I know it is only because he wants to see me play better. We were almost home, coming down a hill, when the car hit black ice. The car started spinning out of control. We came to a jolting rest on a snowbank, but we were both okay.

During that moment, I realized how lucky and how proud I was to have a friend and a father who could get us out of a tight situation and still not care about how he was, but how I was. I never forgot that night. Every time I pass the hill on the way to school, I am still reminded of the night that my dad became my role model and my hero.

Thanh D. Bui
Aquinas High School
Bronx, New York

I'mverysorryalot!

The day was sunny and sweet, just the way she liked it, yet everyone was crying and sad, including me. She wasn't. She was smiling her warm, refreshing smile through the whole thing. Finally it was over, and her smile was covered by the wooden lid. I cried even more. I guess I was afraid I was going to forget her.

I met Eva while visiting my aunt in New Jersey. I was around nine years old. Eva was a very close friend, even considered a relative, of my Aunt Kim. When I first met her, I thought of her as a cheek-pinching old lady. It turned out that she was great fun to be with. While Aunt Kim was showing my parents around the house, Eva snuck me and my sisters and brother into the kitchen. Then she asked, "What would you like to eat?" We couldn't decide, so she suggested liver pâté, chicken feet, tofu, and Limburger cheese. That really cracked us up.

Eva was the first person to teach me how to bake army men cookies and cook worm surprise! She was the kind that would try anything new, even crocodile salad! Actually, the crocodile was green-dyed chicken, the army men cookies were gingerbread men, and worm surprise was actually spaghetti. Whenever we finished our meals she would take the leftovers and feed them to her "dog." She did not really have a dog, but said it anyway. We never got the joke, which made her laugh every time.

44

We started to visit Eva regularly. My aunt wouldn't really mind, but Eva would be anxiously waiting with her baking goods, toys, and library card. Every time we visited, she would either take us to the "enchanting" library or to the small park where she would tell stories about her five children and how much fun they had together. Then, one day while walking to the park, Eva told me that her son Martin died years ago in a motorcycle accident. Eva said she really missed all her children, especially Martin; that's why she played with us all the time. We all fell into a silent pause. She broke the pause with one of her famous jokes.

As I grew older, I visited Eva less and less, until one day she stopped me and asked me why I had ceased visiting. I told her that my friends thought it was kind of weird to hang around an old lady all the time. I immediately regretted what I said because her face grew sad. She said she understood, and before leaving me alone, she said, "Think about what a real friend is." I grew weary with sadness, and decided to apologize Eva-style. So I bought a leash without a dog and went to Eva's house. "This is my dog, his name is I'mverysorryalot!" She laughed and replied, "He must be French." And I knew she forgave me.

Eva grew older and so did I. Then one day she told me that she was moving to New Hampshire to live with her daughter and son-in-law. I suddenly felt so lonely. The day she moved, I tried to hold back my tears when she came up to me. She said, "Don't ever forget me." Then she left smiling that smile of hers.

We wrote frequently to each other, always telling corny jokes. One day, while I was reading one of her letters, I stopped at a sentence and smiled. It read: "Guess what? I finally got a dog!" That was the last letter I received from her.

On the ride home from the funeral, I passed by a small park. I visualized my sisters and brother on the swings and slide, and me talking to Eva on the bench. At that moment I knew I could not forget her.

Sarah Wood
Country Day School
of the Sacred Heart
Bryn Mawr, Pennsylvania

Sunshine

The silence was almost unbearably uncomfortable. I was too nervous to speak, and I think everyone else was too. The car ride seemed endless. Once in a while we would look at each other and force a smile, but our smiles were more nervous than warm.

I don't know what she was thinking about, but I know that memories flooded my head. I was remembering my first day of school when I felt like there was a spotlight shining on me and someone had written "new" on my forehead. She simply looked at me, took my hand, and said, "Come on. I'll help you find your homeroom."

Then there was the time I missed the winning foul shot in a sixth-grade basketball game. The other team was up by one point, and I got fouled just as the buzzer went off. I was allowed one-and-one foul shots, but I missed the first one and the other team won the game. I was angry at myself and apologetic to my team. I felt as though I had let the whole world down. I sat on the bleachers with my head in my hands. Suddenly I felt her hand rest on my shoulder and a flood of warmth and under-standing run through me. When I looked up, she saw how crushed I was and tears came to her eyes. She hugged me and told me the story of when she knocked herself out with her own hockey stick during a game. Laughter quickly overcame my tears.

46

She was also right there when my first boyfriend broke up with me. I was fifteen, but he "wasn't ready for a commitment." As I hung up the phone, I could feel tears suffocating my throat. I felt as though someone had taken my heart away from me in a matter of minutes. But once I was enclosed in her arms, I clung to her as though she was the only thing I had left in the world.

As I came back from my daydreams, I realized that our road trip was almost at its end. Only one hour left. She started twirling her hair like she does when she gets nervous. From the backseat where I was sitting, I saw a single tear roll down her face. It seemed that it took the rest of the car ride for it to reach her chin.

When we drove onto the enormous campus, the rainstorm that had mysteriously appeared was subsiding. We found our way to her assigned dorm, unpacked her things, and were standing at the car about to say our good-byes. I couldn't do it. I couldn't say good-bye. We stared at each other, tears streaming down our faces. One long hug and a kiss on the cheek were our farewell. I climbed into the car and strapped on my seat belt.

She sat down in the grass and watched us pull out of the driveway. I stared through the rearview mirror at my best friend whom I was leaving behind at college. I stared until the car turned the corner and buildings blocked my view of my sister. I looked up into the sky, and through the leftover clouds I saw one single bright ray of sunshine. It was going to be okay.

Gabriela De La Peña
Father Yermo High School
El Paso, Texas

The Friend I Was

My story goes back to when I was in the third grade. I was what they call a follower. I lacked a vivid personality and just went along with whatever my classmates said or did. I've changed now, but I still remember everything that I did and everyone I hurt because of this.

In the third grade, the teacher introduced a new student one day. She was a tall girl with long, brown hair and big, scared eyes. At the beginning, everyone wanted to talk to her and see what she was like. They surrounded her with questions: "What school do you come from?" "Where do you live?" "What's your name?"

This went on for the first few days, but then everything changed. You know how kids are. They'll do something to you, and if you get angry they'll keep on doing it to you just for the pleasure of seeing you get angry. That's exactly what happened to this girl. My classmates and I would make fun of her. She would get angry, and we would all start laughing. It's weird how quickly we found her weakness, and we made her suffer for it.

I'm ashamed to admit that I was one of those who would throw her books on the floor and call her names. We wanted to get rid of her as one wants to get rid of a virus. Every year we would ask her if she was coming back the next year. When she answered "Yes," we would look at each other, roll our eyes, and start groaning. When she answered "No," we would start yelling, and tell her that we were going to have a party to celebrate. She would act as if she didn't care and that our words didn't bother her, but I knew they did. We were all against her. What could she do?

I'll admit that I was sometimes nice to her, when my friends weren't around. I'd talk to her, and we would laugh like old friends. When my friends were around, I'd act like usual and pretend nothing happened. She would try to win my friendship, but I was scared that if I did become her friend, everything that was happening to her would happen to me. I just wasn't the type to take all that. Not everyone would treat her this way. There were some who just kept their mouths shut and neither hurt nor defended her. They just observed everything that happened.

It hurts when I think of all the things that we did to her and of the expression on her face when everyone would sur-round her and tell her things that no one would want to hear. Here I am wanting justice and peace for the world, and I could not even provide it for this girl. It hurts even more when I realize that this girl has become one of my best friends. Even though I treated her like dirt, she is still my friend, and I have a feeling she always will be.

A few months ago, we talked about this period in her life. She told me everything she felt. I asked her to forgive me, and, of course, she did. I feel better now that we have put this behind us and it doesn't linger on top of us like a cloud. I still ask myself whether she has become insecure or become a stronger person because of this. All I can say is that I wish I could go back and do everything all over again. This time I would stand up for her and voice my opinion as loud as I could. I would fight for her, going against all my so-called friends, and do the right thing. I would defend this girl and provide justice and peace for her. I would be the friend I am now and not the friend I was.

I've made my mistakes, but I've learned from them. Now I try to be a better person by not judging people and by learning to understand them. I try to be the light that God wants me to be for others. I know that God is in each of us, and I try to keep this in my mind.

Sara Fogelquist
Holy Names Academy
Seattle, Washington

Gift and Creation

As the daughter of an Episcopal priest, I am in a different situation from most of my peers. Distinguishing my faith from Dad's job has been a challenge, for ecclesiastical politics threatened to overshadow my spirituality. Attempting to separate the two, I began attending Saint Clement's, the neighboring Episcopal parish. Saint Clement's strengthened my faith and deepened my spirituality by teaching me the value of sharing my faith and how to do that. Although I had a supportive group of friends at church and at school, I longed for a personal friend to whom I could relate individually rather than corporately.

A year ago I was given that opportunity. Because my sophomore theology class consisted of only fourteen students, we were able to get to know one another. In the second semester of this class, I was assigned a seat next to Anne. A talented athlete, Anne was someone with whom I thought I had little in common. To my delighted surprise, Anne and I shared the same faith tradition: We were both Episcopalians.

Soon I invited Anne to attend one of my parish's Lenten Fridays. As someone who attended Mass because that was how she had been raised, Anne did not necessarily feel a personal tie to the church. Nonetheless, she did agree to attend the first Lenten Friday. The format was simple: soup supper, class, and stations of the cross. As Lent unfolded, Anne continued coming on Friday nights, not missing one. To my amazement, she and

50

her mother came to my parish's Easter Vigil! I experienced the Resurrection in a new way, for no longer was Anne merely someone I sat beside in theology class. We had become friends! During the Great Fifty Days of Easter and beyond, our friendship blossomed as Anne became a source of encouragement. When ecclesiastical politics at the rectory became more than I could bear, Anne was willing to listen and to attempt to understand. Anne has helped me to know my other friends better, thus making our circle of friends more real.

For my seventeenth birthday last July, Anne organized a surprise party, the first ever given for me. Anne has encouraged me to attend retreats and sports events. Friendship, however, goes two ways—not only what my friend can do for me, but also what I can do for my friend. I have tried to support Anne in her spiritual development. In turn, she has become more involved in her own parish, and she has been selected as one of three campus ministry representatives for our senior class next year. We are able to help each other as we reach out to others.

Last month Anne and I celebrated one year of friendship, the anniversary of that day when she appeared at the first Lenten Friday. As Anne reminisced, "I had no idea what was in store for me by accepting your invitation!" Neither did I! For both of us, acceptance of friendship continues to open new avenues in our journeys of faith. In his book *On Spiritual Friendship*, Saint Aelred, twelfth-century abbot of Rievaulx, wrote that friendship is both a gift from God and a creation of human effort. As we grow spiritually, emotionally, and socially, Anne and I, together with our widening circle of friends, enact Saint Aelred's definition of friendship.

John Donnelly
Marist School
Atlanta, Georgia

Just a Game

On the day of the big game, I woke up to a cool, brisk winter morning. The tip-off for the league championship was at 11:30 a.m. and featured the number one team in the league against my team, ranked fourth. I arrived at the gym and was greeted by one of my best friends. Our team warmed up and stretched as usual. We were physically and mentally ready for the game.

The first half flew by. Before I knew it, I was wiping the sweat off my face as our team ran into the locker room enjoying a 28–20 advantage. I really believed we could get it done. I was almost sure we were going to win. My friend was having a particularly great game. He was playing the best I had ever seen him play.

The game turned into a hard fought, seesaw battle. The third quarter ended in a tie as my friend continued his torrid scoring. He was all over the court. It was almost a virtual dead-lock the rest of the way. With seven seconds left, my team had the ball. We were losing 51–50, so we called a time-out to devise a plan. Since my friend was on fire, we decided to let him have the ball.

We inbounded the ball as the clock ticked :06, :05. He dribbled to the center of the court and blew by the defender. He laid the ball up but missed. The whistle blew. We still had a chance. He had been fouled on the shot. With one second left, his first shot would tie the game, the second could win it. He stepped up to the line. My heart started pounding. The first shot went up, but was no good. My heart started beating faster. The next shot went up, looked good, but just missed to the left. We had lost the game. I was heartbroken, just as I knew my friend was.

After the game, some guys on the team started blaming the loss on my friend. They insulted him and called him names. I walked straight up to him and told him that if it wasn't for his courageous effort we would have never been in the game to begin with. I told him those guys were jerks for putting him down and were just jealous of his abilities. Besides, I added, it was just a game. It wasn't going to affect the rest of his life. It was no big deal. It was over and he had tried his best. That's all he could have done.

I think he felt better after having someone to talk to. I know I do.

Christine Metzger
Villa Joseph Marie
High School
Holland, Pennsylvania

The Bumblebee Girl

She had this swimsuit, black and yellow striped, with small iridescent wings stitched to the back. In one of the earliest pictures I have of her, she's wearing her bumblebee suit and her sand-dusted hand is stretched out to the camera. In her palm is a sand crab, the kind seen when a wave recedes into the sea, exposing hundreds of tiny, wiggling creatures. Her sunburnt nose is wrinkled in obvious disgust. The wind is blowing her sun-bleached hair across her face as she squints in the summer light. When I think of Julie, I often remember her as this incarnation, as the Bumblebee Girl.

We met at the YMCA when we were one or two years old, taking swimming classes there. Our mothers were forced into friendship because Julie and I were the only two children who would throw tantrums if so much as one molecule of water touched our precious baby skin. I went to her second birthday party, and even after the atrocities I committed there, throwing up on the table and on her bed, she still liked me. Our friendship has always worked that way—except I haven't thrown up on any of her personal belongings lately.

When we were in early elementary school, she lived in an apartment, and we would go hang out on the laundry room steps and talk about our five years on earth. She had Billy, I had Mikey, and we were happy and perfectly content. We did not go to the same school and lived several miles away from each other. The time between our visits seemed immense, and we harassed our mothers with pleading, teary faces crying, "Just five more minutes, please?"

After living at the apartments for several years, Julie and her mother moved into her grandmother's house, which was always neat to visit because they had a kidney-shaped, in-ground pool and a big, life-size Barbie head that swiveled so you could do its hair and makeup.

Then Julie and her mother moved to 15 Velvet Lane, their current residence. For a few weeks after the move, they didn't have a lawn mower, and we played safari in the overgrown backyard and camped out under the kitchen table.

As we grew up, we went through phases together, most noticeable in our lavender, then tropical fish room decor. Even our gifts usually matched during the holidays. Julie called me Christmas morning, sixth grade, to shriek: "Christine! I got it! A phone! My own phone! It's blue and it lights up!" I, of course, had to call her right back on my brand-spanking-new, pink light-up phone.

We wore matching outfits and were convinced we could pass as twins. With our dark hair, skin, and eyes, it worked a surprising number of times. Our whole Girl Scout camp thought we were sisters for several days at the beginning of the summer that we went there. Even though she cried in the bathroom a lot and even though they made her go canoeing, I know Julie had a good time. I would sneak over to her bunk after lights out, and we would eat jelly beans in silence, listening to the creaking night, and sometimes to Julie's homesick sniffling.

Girl Scouts brought us together because in our home troop we were united against a common enemy: Marie, our troop leader. Our general ignorance of authority was a result of the dislike we felt was mutual between us and Marie. At every meeting we created at least a small, innocent ruckus. Julie and I stood by each other, from the time we used all of Marie's dish soap on the Slip-N-Slide at a picnic to when we accidentally pushed the screen out of Marie's window. In the former incident, we got yelled at and I got a really nasty case of contact dermatitis, but Julie and I had a good laugh over calamine lotion. In the latter, we had been making friendship bracelets at a meeting, and Julie and I got the grand idea to put some string on the window ledge for birds to use for nesting. Well, needless to say, the idea wasn't so grand, and when Marie saw the screen on her driveway and the two of us in tearful hysterics on her floor, she told us never to return to Girl Scouts. Getting in trouble is never fun without an accomplice and, with no disrespect for the Girl Scouts of America intended, Julie has always been the best.

We are on the same odd wavelength and sometimes it's scary. We can finish each other's sentences, and we often call each other at the same time. Julie is one of the few people I can truly be a child with. Even though she had just turned seventeen, we played dress-up not too long ago. It was a rainy Sunday, and her storage room beckoned us with its stuffed closet: a bear costume, three different bridesmaid's dresses, two wedding dresses, several halter tops, a witch/vampire cape, princess gear (tiara, scepter, and pink crinoline skirts), assorted animal noses, and a pair of sunglasses that change color in sunlight. On a road trip recently, we wore plastic bag hats (we're easily entertained) and scared a good percentage of our fellow travelers on the PA Turnpike. The fact that we can act childish with no fear of social repercussions is a great relief.

We once talked of how we would live together in an apartment and work part-time at Dunkin' Donuts. She would be a Mexican chef, and I was going to be a ballerina–fashion designer–nun. I don't have any clear idea of what I want to be anymore, but Julie is a constant reminder of who I have become. I'll probably name my first daughter after her and she'll be the first person I call when I get the phone line connected in a new house when we're separated by miles or more. And Julie, no matter how far away she is, will always be my Bumblebee Girl.

Jayme Perry
Chaminade Julienne High School
Dayton, Ohio

Megan Bliznik
Aquinas High School
La Crosse, Wisconsin

Alive in My Heart

I lived in Japan from sixth grade to my freshman year in high school. My father had accepted a job with the government. Of course, I was extremely apprehensive about the move. When we got there, I didn't know anyone.

I met my first friend at the clinic when I was getting vaccinations for school. Her name was Jeni. She was a year older than me and extremely pretty. It just so happened that Jeni had also just moved to Japan and didn't know anyone either. I was so happy when she introduced herself. As we started talking, we realized that we had a lot in common. When it came time for me to leave, we exchanged phone numbers. I was both excited and relieved to have a friend in the same boat as me.

No sooner did I walk in the door at home than the phone rang. It was Jeni! This was the beginning of a strong friendship. We did everything together: went to movies, had sleepovers, and had serious talks about life. She told me her dreams, and I told her mine. When school started, we didn't see as much of each other, but still remained friends and did things together. Two years passed by so quickly. I was in eighth grade and Jeni was a freshman.

One weekend I was just being lazy watching TV when my mom came in to tell me that Jeni was in intensive care at the hospital. She had been at a friend's house on a different military base when she'd had an asthma attack. Her friend's mom immediately got her in the car to take her to the hospital that was at least ten minutes away. On the way there, the car broke down. Jeni went into a coma.

I wanted to go see Jeni, but never got the chance. I truly believed that she would be fine. But Jeni lost her battle.

So what is this saying about friends? Value them. I never got the chance to tell Jeni how much I loved and cared for her. Two years ago I went to Arlington to visit her grave. I wish that I had gotten the chance to tell Jeni, not a grave. Jeni is alive in my heart today. I still talk to her every Sunday. I have learned how precious life and friendship really are.

Miriam Harris
Our Lady of the Elms
High School
Akron, Ohio

Send Me
a True Friend

I remember myself as a small child sitting on the swings, alone on the school playground. I had few friends, and the ones I had, unfortunately, lacked loyalty. Every night I would kneel down at my bed and pray the very same prayer: "Dear Lord, I'm so lonely. Could you please send me a true friend? I need a friend now more than anything." The next morning I would wake up and ride the bus to school. Again I heard the insults of the kids I called my friends.

"You're fat," Samantha would tell me. "How much do you weigh?"

I answered her with a lie about my weight because she was so much thinner than me and weighed such a small amount.

"Where do you buy your clothes?" Teresa would inquire. "They are so ugly. Didn't you wear that shirt last week?"

I never answered Teresa. I knew some of my clothes weren't as pretty as hers.

At lunch, Anna would comment on my lunch: "Don't you ever have anything healthy in your lunch? All you have is junk food! You're going to die when you get older because of all that fat!"

Every night I returned home upset, yet holding in my pain and frustration where it burned away at my heart. One night I made the grim connection: "If only I was as thin and pretty as Samantha, maybe the kids would accept me."

60

From that night on, I strove for my goal. I eliminated fat from my diet and began to exercise. This continued and eventually led years later to more extreme ways to lose weight. I never became extremely emaciated, but my heart starved evermore for an intimate friend. I continued to pray, at this point also searching for a soul to trust with my eating problems.

One night at a church meeting, Peter, just an acquaintance at the time, approached me. "You look like you need someone to talk to," he said. A smile formed on my face. Although I hardly knew him, I felt safe enough to tell him how alone and dejected I felt.

During the next few months I told more and more to Peter. He was there just to listen to me. At that time I never returned the favor by listening to his problems. Honestly, I had not the ability to be a friend in return. I'm grateful he was patient and understanding enough for me to learn how to give back the love and friendship he gave me.

I learned much about myself through Peter. I came to the realization that I would be in serious medical trouble if I went without help for my eating disorder. Peter did not tell on me, but rather waited until I yearned for help myself. Even then, knowing I was fearful of exposing the problem, he asked my permission to tell the pastor of our church.

To this day, I thank Peter for the support he's given me. I would still be without help for my eating disorder today if he hadn't been there for me during my tough times. I don't think I could find a more caring, compassionate, and trustworthy friend. Peter is exactly what I had been praying for all those years.

Rachel Pierce
Academy of the Holy Names
Albany, New York

Her Name Was Betty

I remember the day I was assigned to her for confirmation class about two years ago. About thirteen restless teenagers were squashed into the basement of our instructor's house, all itching to leave. We had just received a paper discussing our latest service project. Across from each of our names on a list was the name of a senior citizen living in a nursing home. This person was to become our pen pal and the recipient of a few of our gifts. Most of the kids in my class groaned at this new assignment, but I didn't. I didn't look at this as just another project, but as a mission. I had the chance to bring happiness into the life of a stranger, to bring a smile to the face of a lonely woman.

Her name was Betty. She had no family and hadn't had a visitor in years. Her room was sparsely decorated and her possessions few. Also, because of serious ailments, she was housebound. I began writing to Betty as a stranger, then as a friend. I eagerly awaited some sort of a response, but I soon found out I would not be receiving one because Betty suffered from crippling arthritis in her hands. At first I was disappointed, but I realized it wouldn't matter as long as she could receive my letters. Even though I wouldn't be receiving letters from her, I did receive something inside.

Christmas arrived, and I sent my new friend a present I knew she'd appreciate: a pink, fuzzy robe. Now I could warm her heart and the rest of her. I later heard from the manager of the nursing home that the robe was, in fact, greatly appreciated. Betty barely ever took off the robe; it was her pride and joy. Just knowing that I had brought even a small amount of cheer into another's life made me happy.

I continued writing to Betty and sending her festive cards on the holidays. I tried to arrange a visit, but rules of privacy that were associated with this project kept me from it. Once during the project, the manager of the nursing home came to talk to us and show us slides of our seniors. When she was flipping through the slides, I immediately recognized Betty. She was wearing the robe I gave her and a smile from ear to ear. Underneath it all, however, was a frail, sickly woman with much suffering in her eyes. I like to think that I put that smile on her face, that I was her friend.

Confirmation classes soon ended, but I didn't stop writing. I was determined to keep Betty smiling.

This October I received word that Betty had passed away after a period of illness. I never got to meet my friend, but it felt good knowing that I had filled the last two years of her life with sunshine.

Holly Melzer
Bishop Hartley High School
Columbus, Ohio

Cincinnati

Vanessa and I met at dance class six years ago and have been close friends ever since. She lives in Gahanna, I live in Reynoldsburg, and with our busy social lives we see each other less and less. We used to have to badger our parents for rides to each other's house. We couldn't wait until we got our licenses, so we could drive places ourselves. We joked around about driving to Cincinnati just for the fun of it with her radio blaring and windows rolled down, hair blowing in the breeze.

At first we had talked a few times, but I wouldn't say we were friends. I begged my mom to drop me off early and pick me up late so I could watch Vanessa dance. I sat on the floor with my nose pressed against the window, watching in admiration. She could do a triple pirouette in a third of a second. I got dizzy just watching her whirl around the room like a top that had just been let loose. I adored Vanessa.

When I was in sixth grade and Vanessa was in seventh, I picked her as my "big sister" for dance lines. She bought me the best presents and wrote me little notes spontaneously to make me feel better. She curled my hair at competitions, taught me how to put on makeup without looking like a clown, and how to talk to guys. She listened to my stories about my latest crushes. Most of all, she was always there when I needed her.

I moved up to her dance lines and classes, so we saw each other all the time. We became best friends. I lived at her house

64

on weekends and vacations. We shared everything. We had half of our clothes in each other's closet, and toothbrushes in each other's bathroom. We told each other everything and went through so much together.

One day my mom dropped us off at Vanessa's house; we could hear her parents shouting before we even opened the door. Vanessa, a little embarrassed, turned a slight shade of red. I flashed a smile, grabbed their mail, and followed her quietly into her room where we sat for hours, ignoring the arguing and occasional shouts that came from the kitchen. Her parents never realized we had come in. We were lying on her bed when her dad yelled, "I want a divorce!" and her mom screamed, "Great!" I hugged weeping Vanessa, her lips moving silently with the word "divorce."

Vanessa spent that night at my house. We had stayed up late, so when my mom came in my room at 5:00 a.m. and turned the lights on, we were confused. All I heard was "Going to the hospital" as my mom closed the door.

Finally around 9:00 a.m., we heard the garage door open. Vanessa turned off the Bugs Bunny cartoon that we weren't really watching. We stared fearfully at each other. Mom walked slowly through the door, hung up her coat, and looked at us both, "Grandma died." Vanessa wrapped her arms around me, both of us with tears streaming down our face.

We're always there when we need each other most. Going to different schools has strained our friendship, but we've been through too much to throw it away because of a few inconveniences. We talk on the phone often and go out on weekends.

Vanessa still does little things to surprise me. Saturday she called at 9:00 a.m., saying she was coming over. When she arrived, I jumped in the car. "Where to?" I screamed above the blaring radio. "Cincinnati," she answered, laughing. I smiled as she peeled out of my driveway, our hair blowing in the breeze.

Penelope Love Vlanos
Fenwick High School
Oak Park, Illinois

Yiayia

As I stood next to my grandmother's beautiful, cherry wood coffin, holding her cold, lifeless hand, I wept. This was not how I remembered her. She was neither lifeless nor cold, but rather, full of life and vitality. Yiayia, the Greek word for grandmother, was the most beautiful person I knew. From looking at her in her coffin, one could surely see that she was a very pretty woman, but her inner beauty was far deeper.

I sat there talking to Yiayia about our wonderful times together. Of course I was speaking in Greek because Yiayia did not speak English very well, and therefore she would not have understood me. Our ability to communicate in Greek strengthened our relationship and made it unique. Often, if one of us did not understand the other, we would play charades. This was quite humorous because we would both end up laughing hysterically, not even remembering what we were trying to act out. Yiayia began teaching me Greek when I was first born. Now I can speak and write in Greek rather fluently.

When Yiayia slept over at our house she always slept with me in my bed, not because there was no extra bed for her, but simply because we loved each other's company. When I came into bed, she was always waiting up for me. We cuddled up together, and she wrapped her warm feet around my cold ones and rubbed them until they were toasty warm. Often we embraced each other for a long time before finally falling asleep.

66

We talked about everything. Yiayia was always there for me, and we trusted each other with our deepest secrets. She taught me Greek poems, songs, and prayers, and told me Greek myths. Yiayia taught me all the things that her mother taught her, and her mother's mother taught her, and so on. She passed her Greek heritage down to me.

I remember when I was younger and Yiayia wore a pink sundress with a big watermelon collar that was a favorite of mine. She used to tell me that if I swallowed watermelon seeds, a watermelon tree would grow in my tummy. We took walks to the park, and she sang songs to me while she pushed me on the swings. On our way home, without fail, a freight train always passed, and we counted the number of train cars.

I can still smell the wonderful aroma of mouthwatering French toast that I used to wake up to at Yiayia's house. Yiayia was the best cook, but I never understood how everything tasted so delicious when she never measured anything. Yiayia simply knew how much of everything was needed to make it perfect.

I recall sitting at the kitchen table with Yiayia teaching me how to wrap a ball of ground beef in a leaf to make a special Greek food of hers. I was never able to get it quite right and the leaf always broke, but Yiayia pretended that mine were perfect, even better than hers.

And I remember my last words to Yiayia just before she died. I squeezed her hand and whispered into her ear: "Yiayia, thank you for everything. You are my best friend in the world. I will always remember you, and I love you."

Jim Guth
Holy Redeemer High School
Detroit, Michigan

Sis

A friendship is a very good thing. What I am about to tell you now is a very personal story about my cousin and her friend. My cousin's name is Helena, but we all call her Sis. Her friend's name is Jennifer.

My cousin Sis and her friend Jennifer have been friends for as long as I can remember. They fight and argue; like any other friends, they have their disagreements. It is perfectly normal for friends to do that, right? But no matter what happens, they always seem to overcome their problems and remain best friends. In their eyes they are sisters, and from what I see and what anybody else sees, it's not hard to believe.

Well, to get to the point, about four years ago, when my cousin and her friend were juniors in high school, they were invited to a senior graduation party, but only because they knew people. The party was near a bridge in Taylor, Michigan. Beneath the bridge were abandoned railroad tracks from about fifty years ago. Some abandoned boxcars remained as well. About twenty to thirty feet of water had risen above the tracks in those fifty or so years.

At the party, a bunch of the people became intoxicated, even my cousin's friend Jennifer. But Sis and a couple of her friends did not drink. Well, Jennifer was so intoxicated that she did not know her own name. A couple of the seniors got together and dared her to jump off the bridge naked. A guy said that if she did it he would give her a hundred dollars. So Jennifer began taking off her clothes, getting ready to jump.

A girl who was sober ran to get my cousin to stop Jennifer from jumping. Sis ran as fast as she could to get up to the bridge and stop her best friend. By the time Sis got to the top of the bridge, Jennifer was on the railing of the bridge, ready to jump. My cousin dove at Jennifer in order to knock her down. When Sis grabbed Jennifer, she was mad and still wanted to jump.

If my cousin had not been there, Jennifer would have probably killed herself. I say "killed" because a couple of hours later a guy jumped off the bridge and hit the train underneath. The water split his arm open all the way down his side and broke it in three places. If he had jumped where Jennifer was going to, he would have landed directly on the train and killed himself.

After Jennifer saw that, she realized my cousin—her best friend—had saved her life. She is grateful, and listens to my cousin when she knows Sis is right. And Sis listens to Jennifer when she knows Jennifer is right. To me, that is a perfect friendship: someone who will risk her life to save a friend.

Naoimh O'Connor
Heywood Community School
Portaoise, Laois, Ireland

Everywhere but Near Me

Dear Friend,

It is almost dawn. The sky behind the mountains is changing from black to gray, blue to silver. The world below lies in total silence. Then, high on a stunted birch, a small bird begins to sing. As if in answer to the sweet melody, the sun bounces up in a bright red hat and the sky flames crimson. On cue, the world bursts forth into full, glorious color.

I smile. We haven't slept all night. We're seated on our luggage outside the old, grey-stone farmhouse that's been our home for the past three weeks. We're singing softly the songs we learned, or just the ones we already knew. It's quiet, but there's no apprehension. No tension. All fourteen of us. Singing softly in the sunrise.

Less than a month ago, we came here as individuals or small groups to learn to speak our native language, Irish, with greater fluidity and confidence. Now we're leaving, and we know how to speak the language of our hearts with all the ease of butter on a hot pan. I cannot stop the tears from falling, my heart from sinking, or my words from numbing.

I have never felt so strong a feeling of desolation before. This is because, when I am with all of you, I cannot remember so strong an emotion of sheer elation, the simple joy of being around you. They, whoever they are, say to fully understand either desolation or elation, one must first fully experience both.

Before I thought this was a clever old proverb, but time makes us wise. Now I have experienced both, and I can understand either.

Our destination is beautiful: the scenery, the fresh scent of the salty sea, the sprawling patchwork quilt of green, the rolling hills and dales, the soft breeze, the sight of the sinking ball of fire at sunset. However, I would be inclined to think that the most beauteous sights here are seated around me. Those complaining of sunburned, aching limbs, applying makeup, shouting for hair-tongs. The bus arrives to bring us to join everybody else.

There, I see you. Your face, your smile, your accent. They won't leave my mind. Images of the times we've spent together—talking, walking, being—refuse to depart. I take your hand. The lump in my throat prevents words. Our lips meet momentarily. There is understanding. You are laughing and joking, fully aware that within three or four hours we'll be on opposite ends of the country. You also know that if you don't laugh, you'll join me in tears.

For anyone who's never spent twenty-odd days in the company of so many young people at one time, eating together, sleeping in the same room, partaking in activities together, being together, I'm sure the very concept of sinking into a deep state of melancholy because of separation is entirely alien. Often, those we go to school with, work with, or even speak to on the bus are classified as friends, not due to choice, but to necessity. Those you spend each working day with see only the amount of you that you wish to expose. And because you are constantly changing, it is often difficult for them to accept you.

This year I learned something—something so valuable it can't be bought, so intricate it can't be understood, and yet so simple. It is beautiful. I learned the true meaning of friendship—the accepting of beings for who they are. Fate threw us together. It tore us apart too, but it left us with a lesson, and a bountiful supply of memories to help us through times when we feel unable to look at life as anything but a bleak, dreary substitute for death.

I know a lot of people—acquaintances. Each new day introduces me to a new face, a new personality. But friends are born, they are not made. That is why all those I can call close to me live everywhere but near me.

Name Withheld
Immaculate High School
Danbury, Connecticut

People Like Stars

Sara and I are best friends. We've known each other for about twelve years. Actually, we're closer than best friends; we're like sisters. We know everything about each other, down to shoe size. Sara's the kind of person you can go to if you have a problem or if you just want some company. She's always in a good mood, always finding ways to entertain herself and her friends.

Last year things started to change. We slowly grew apart from each other. I didn't know why. It seemed as though she was mad at me, but I wasn't sure. When I would ask her what was wrong, she would snap at me and say, "Nothing." I figured that she needed time to herself, without me. We slowly stopped calling each other and spending time together. We wouldn't talk much in school, and I felt as though I had done something mean to her.

Every time I thought about what I could have done to make her upset, I ended up sad and completely confused. This went on for about four months. That's when I started noticing that something was wrong. She had lost an unbelievable amount of weight. Her legs were like toothpicks, and her arms were like spaghetti. She had no stomach, and her face was like a ghost, barely there.

I wondered how she had lost so much weight. That's when it hit me: she had stopped eating lunch and said she never ate breakfast. I was incredibly worried. I almost cried when I finally realized what she was doing. She was starving herself.

So one day after school I showed up at her house. She was shocked, but I told Sara I really needed to talk to her. When I told her that I knew what she was doing, she became annoyed and didn't like the fact that I knew. She kept denying it, and said she was fine. I knew she wasn't. I had to do something.

I kept bugging her about it, and one day she finally blew up at me about it. Sara said that it wasn't my problem, it was hers, and nobody cared about her anyway. Tears ran from her eyes. She cried and cried. Without any question, I put my arms around her and began to comfort her. She kept on saying: "I hate this, what am I doing to myself? Why, why?"

When she finally caught her breath, I asked her why she was starving herself. The tears began to roll down her face again, and she began to tell me. She said that her parents had been fighting a lot lately, her grades were slipping, and her boyfriend was always putting her down, saying that she was ugly and too fat.

We both knew she wasn't. She had been a healthy one hundred and eighteen pounds. Now she was ninety-six pounds. I was completely shocked that she was dealing with these problems. I couldn't believe that I, her best friend, was so completely oblivious to her problems.

After she had told me everything, she said, "Sorry."

I said: "For what? You have nothing to be sorry about." But Sara replied: "Yes, I do. I'm sorry I drifted away from my friend, my best friend." That's when I cried and realized how much we missed each other.

We both knew she needed help. The next day she and her mom went to see a nutritionist. Now things are getting back to normal. She has gained four pounds, and she's trying her hardest to deal with her problems in a healthy way.

I guess it took something this big to make us both realize how strong and special our friendship is. But there's always going to be a bigger lesson in this story for me. I learned that people are like stars. At night when you look up at the sky, you see a few stars. If you look closer, you may see more of them. And if you look as closely as you can, you'll see that each star has it's own light—some brighter than others, shining in their own way. But no matter how hard you try or how close you look, you'll never know everything about the stars. You're just blinded by their light.

Jessica Wagner
Chaminade Julienne
High School
Dayton, Ohio

Rachel
Lancaster Catholic
High School
Lancaster, Pennsylvania

Where Is She?

Shelly and I met in second grade, and within a year we were inseparable. For years, a week would not pass that we didn't sleep over with each other. No secrets existed between us. We were like sisters. The same clothes, hair, cassette tapes, and crushes were part of our very special and unique bond.

Junior high arrived and, with it, many problems. Shelly had decided that her straight A's and special classes at a local college were of limited importance to her growing social calendar. Another girl, Marie, had joined our group and brought with her boys, drinking, and smoking. Shelly mirrored the company she kept. When she was with me, she acted the way I did. But in Marie's company she was a different person, certainly not my best friend of four years.

Difficult periods played a major role in our last two years in elementary school. We made it to high school with a distant and weak bond between us. Marie attended a different school. Reacquainted during freshman year, the sisterly love blossomed once again. The pain of our past separation gradually subsided until our friendship suddenly and violently ended during junior year.

Shelly's grades had been dropping for some time when she finally hit an all-time low—only three passing grades. Her circle of friends expanded to include drug addicts, drug suppliers, boys with police records, and girls who fought for fun. Her entire aura changed. Smiling was rare, and her appearance deteriorated rapidly. My shy, sweet best friend was getting tested for AIDS, stealing, running away, and getting high.

I loved her so much that I wanted to help her. I just wanted Shelly to come back, but she couldn't find the way. The more involved I was, the further away she drifted. Until she was gone. She dropped out of school, was living in a one-room apartment with one of her many boyfriends, and spent more days high than not. Shelly's mom and stepdad had given up. They could not watch her twenty-four hours a day.

The girl that sat on my bed and held me as I cried about my parent's divorce was now living a nightmare herself. In tears, she called me maybe a dozen times over the next ten months. Rape, pregnancy, black eyes, it didn't matter what it was, she still wouldn't allow me to help. Rehab hadn't helped, so she decided to accept her hell and live within it.

Where is Shelly now? I'm not sure. I hear stories about her being with different boys or men around town, but she's stopped calling.

Shelly will always be my best friend. She's going to be my maid of honor at my wedding and the godmother of my first-born. My only hope is that she's alive and someday finds her way home.

Brian Egan
La Salle College
High School
Wyndmoor, Pennsylvania

Burns and Bruises

I met Mike the first day of kindergarten. We were assigned by the school to carpool with each other, along with two girls, Dara and Amanda. My mother was driving that day, and we had just picked up the two girls. The girls were dressed very nicely, though they had those stupid colored bows in their hair that mothers thought were adorable looking.

We then pulled into Mike's driveway, only to be greeted by ducks, chickens, goats, and dogs. All these animals ran in circles around the car, making enough noise to shatter the windows. The place smelled like crap. Mike came out of the house and got into the backseat of my car. Luckily my mom was driving so I was in the front seat, because the stench of Mike's barnyard carried right onto his clothes.

He evidently didn't go shopping for school clothes, and his face and hair were so dirty that I convinced myself that he was so poor that he didn't own a shower. I also noticed black spots up and down his arms and an occasional black-and-blue mark, but I thought nothing of them. Once he started talking, he seemed like a nice boy, but very timid when we asked him personal questions. We finally arrived at school and attended our first day of education. Mike got along with everybody, but he was very rough at times, even hitting a kid when he didn't share a toy with him.

The days went by repetitively. I looked forward to Tuesdays and Fridays when my mother drove so I could lay claim to the front seat. On the other days, I made sure to get a window seat because I knew Mike would have the other window seat. One day I even had to go inside Mike's house with my mother for some reason. I can't say that inside was any better. Actually it was worse, because no fresh air mingled with the stench of bird crap. Birds flew everywhere in his house, and a layer of smog had formed around Mike's chain-smoking mother. He didn't have a father. He lived with his grandfather and mother. Once Mike was ready to go, I ran as fast as I could for the front seat, dodging every pile of crap lying in the yard. I later told my mother, "I never want to go inside there again."

I felt bad for Mike, though. He always had these bruises all over his body and burnt skin all over his arms. I would ask him about it from time to time. I had never heard of someone falling down the steps and landing on the oven burner as many times as Mike had. For reasons I did not understand at the time, my mom always told me to be nice to Mike and to invite him over to our house. Mike was always very happy to come, and tears gathered in the corners of his eyes when my mom would say it was time to go. It took me a few months until I got the guts to ask my mom what was wrong with Mike.

"Mom, why does Mike always have bruises and burns on his arms?"

"I don't want you to repeat this, but I think he may be abused."

I was a kindergartner. How am I supposed to repeat stuff with words longer than three letters?

"Well, what are the black spots on his arms?"

"Those are most probably cigarette burns. His mother probably gets angry at him and burns him with cigarettes."

That was the biggest lie I had ever heard. Why would a parent put a cigarette on their kid's arm if they have an ashtray? This whole idea of abuse baffled me. I did gather, though, that Mike's mother did bad things to him for reasons that I did not know. Whenever I saw Mike's mother I wanted to say something to her about hurting Mike, but I thought she would hurt me too.

I went through the year without opening my mouth, but every so often I heard, "I fell down the steps and landed on the burner right after my mom turned it on." I thought that was the coolest story, because even though I could fall down the steps, the burner half of Mike's incidents never happened to me. I was envious of him for that.

At the end of the year, Mike told me that he was moving. At first I was happy because I wouldn't have to worry about the front seat, but then I felt very sad. What would happen to Mike? Would his mother ever be nice to him? I often heard my mother talking with the two girls' mothers about Mike. They all had the same feelings, but they never said anything to anyone but one another.

Mike and his family were moving and I could do nothing to save Mike. My mother asked Mike's mother to keep in touch, but Mike's mother never told us where they were moving and never gave us their phone number. Mike was gone.

I am sixteen now. I always wonder what happened to Mike. For all I know, he could be dead. Why couldn't I have innocently said something to Mike's mother about the problem? I want to blame myself, but my mother never made an attempt to say anything either. If the abuse had been stopped, Mike would have been able to enjoy life. Instead, Mike was, and still is, on his own. It didn't have to be that way.

I have to ask myself the question, Was I really a friend to Mike? He obviously showed great respect for me by playing with me and treating me well when he came to play. I was one of the few who actually ignored the stench to try to be friendly. I have to consider the naïveté of a kindergarten student. Obviously, I knew no better. My only hope today is that Mike, wherever he may be, can look back at kindergarten and consider me to be one of his friends.

Virginia Prochilo
Bishop Kearney
High School
Brooklyn, New York

Michele Gullotti
Country Day School
of the Sacred Heart
Bryn Mawr, Pennsylvania

Together Always

A friendship I will remember for the rest of my life began in a preschool classroom in Overbrook. Eight of the total ten children in the class were at one table; I was seated at table two, and she sat down at table three. The teacher passed out crayons and coloring books. We all grabbed them like they were candy. During the first few minutes of coloring time, the two of us glanced at each other sitting similarly alone. Finally, yet somewhat abruptly, she got up from her table, picked up her crayons and coloring book, and came and sat down next to me.

"Hi, my name's Jacqui. Are you shy?"

"Yeah, kinda," I responded.

"What's your name?"

"Michele."

"Never met anyone named 'Michele' before."

"Really?"

"Your favorite color's pink, right?"

"Yeah, how did you . . ."

She pointed at my paper. The page I had been halfheartedly coloring for the past few minutes contained three Sesame Street characters. They appeared to be dripping in Pepto-Bismol. Discovering what I had done, I turned my attention to her artwork. To my enjoyment, the pair of turtles on her page were pink.

"Yeah, me too," she said as she caught my smile.

And then we laughed. It was during this first of many smiles that I knew I had a friend.

82

For the next two years we were always together and always smiling. We shared our lunches, played games together, sang songs, and always shared our pink crayons.

Then one night everything changed. I can't clearly remember my dream from that night, but I do remember waking in the middle of the night from the cry of the telephone and feeling tears run down my face. I put my hand on my pink pillow and felt that it was damp. Unsure of the cause of my tears, I assumed it was a scary dream and hesitantly fell back to sleep; I didn't want to be tired for school.

But the next morning my mother didn't wake me in time for the bus. Instead, I awoke and saw that it was 10:30 a.m. I left my room, still in my pink pajamas, to question my mother's omission. I found her in the kitchen sobbing, with her head hidden in my father's shoulder. I didn't know what to think.

"What's wrong?" I said, forgetting my original question. Unaware of me until that moment, my mother turned abruptly toward me and sat down at the table. She wiped her eyes on her sleeve and motioned for me to come closer. I climbed into her lap, and she hugged me. She then delivered the news.

"Last night, umm . . . ah . . . well . . . Jacqui and her mother were in a car accident. They were hit by another car, and . . ." She tried to continue, but instead of words came more tears, and she simply hugged me.

My father finished, "They're both with God, Honey."

After a few more questions, followed by sobbing answers, I went back to my room and sat on my bed. From this seat I could see myself in the mirror, wrapped in my pink blanket. But as I looked harder, it wasn't my brown hair reflecting back, but Jacqui's blond. They weren't my brown, tear-filled eyes, but her green ones. I no longer saw a shy little girl with many reservations, but a confident one with aspirations.

Now that I look back, I realize that Jacqui gave me a seed of confidence that would continue to grow as I did. She helped me to become more outgoing and talkative. Many times I have wondered what we would be doing today if she were here with me. But then I look in the mirror and realize that she is with me. And that part of me that is her will not only help me grow, but will accompany me throughout my life.

Jordan E. Walsh
Mount Saint Joseph Academy
Flourtown, Pennsylvania

A Friend in Need

I have always considered myself a person who has many friendly acquaintances, but not many true friends. I have always needed many people and activities going on in my life at one time, but because there is so much going on, I never really felt that anyone considered me a close friend. That is, until my father's heart attack and surgery this past November. I've always heard that you judge your friends by who stands by you when things are all wrong, not when things are going well.

Three days after my father had his heart attack, everything seemed to be going very well, so the surgeons decided to remove the balloon pump that had been pumping my father's heart for him. Murphy's law. Almost immediately after the pump was removed, my father went into distress and began to show signs of another heart attack.

One of my mom's coworkers picked me up early from school and took me to the hospital. When we got there, I found out that they were going to have to do emergency surgery on my dad. To make it worse, they weren't even going to do it until the next afternoon because they had to wait twenty-four hours after the trauma my father's heart had been through earlier that day. I tried to stay calm, but it wasn't working very well.

I lost control completely when the surgeon began describing the procedure. Six, possibly seven bypasses? I left the ICU and went out to the waiting room. I went over to the pay phone and called one of my best friends, Lauren. She knew that my dad was in the hospital, but that morning I had told her everything was going well. She cried with me. Then she told me that she was going to have her dad drive her to the hospital, no matter what the ICU visitor regulations were. I was relieved. Then, two minutes later the waiting room phone rang. It was another of my friends, Gina. Lauren had called her and told her what had happened. All she said was, "I'm coming."

I can still remember seeing them get off the elevator. I ran down the hall, hugged them, and cried. Another one of my friends, Tiffany, with whom I had recently lost touch, had come with them. She said that she had heard from a mutual friend and just had to be there. They decided to take me out to dinner to get my mind off of things.

We went to this little diner a few blocks from the hospital. The food wasn't great, but I think it was the best dinner I've ever had. We just sat and talked, reminisced and laughed, something I hadn't done in about four days. I know it might seem selfish to want people there for me when my dad was the one in danger and need, but I did need them. It made me feel good to know that these people cared about me enough to drive forty-five minutes from home on a school night to be there for me. I couldn't believe it when they said two more of my friends, Rebecca and Colleen, had wanted to come but weren't allowed.

Mr. Smith, Lauren's father, drove me home that night, and shortly after I got home, my mom, aunt, and grandmother arrived. It was then that I realized I wasn't going to be able to handle the next day alone. So at 11:30 p.m., I called the Smith's. I asked Lauren if she could miss school the next day to come to the hospital with me. She didn't even think twice. "What time are we leaving?" she asked.

I don't know if I could have made it through that day without Lauren. She was there when I broke down because my uncle, who is also our lawyer, came to have my dad re-sign his will, and when the priest came in to give my dad last rites— even though they are not called that anymore. When my dad finally went into surgery at two o'clock, we knew the worst had just begun.

Seven hours of waiting followed. Lauren sat with me, talked to me, played cards with me, and made me laugh. At 9:30 that night, the surgeon came out and said the best words I've ever heard: "Everything went very well." Lauren knew to just let my mom and I cry with each other. That is what true friends are for.

Ashley Goodman
Holy Cross High School
Louisville, Kentucky

Quintress M. Leslie
Mount de Sales Academy
Macon, Georgia

Dreaming Miracles

The huge helmet with a glossy number 72 painted on its side hit the ground with a thud as my brother Thomas, my best friend, brought down the other team's quarterback. With just three seconds left in the game, he'd sacked the crucial member of the state's number one ranked high school football team, preventing them from scoring a touchdown. We had won the championship!

I dreamed about that night happily, and saw myself as one of a thousand screaming fans rushing the field with hysterical congratulations. They hoisted Thomas on their shoulders, the hero of the day. While everyone rejoiced in one of the greatest upsets in football history, I delighted in my own private victories, looking at number 72. It was a very happy time for me. In my sleep, my neck brace began to itch.

I remember lying in a puddle, thoroughly soaked and very dizzy, one cold February night. I squinted hard and made out the dark shapes surrounded by white light to be a video store sign, a lamppost, and a small, mangled, blue Toyota that had lost the shine it had had only minutes before. It looked like an old soda can that had been stomped and forgotten. My first car accident had been a nightmare.

I had been driving home during a bad thunderstorm and had stopped at a red light when a deafening crash bumped me through a busy intersection and up a hill. My car, which luckily missed all oncoming traffic, spun to a sloshy stop on the road-side, the force snapping my head backwards over the headrest. As I struggled to free myself from the seatbelt, I came to the most horrible realization I'd ever known. My brother and some friends had been following me home that night. He was in the car that hit me!

I jumped from the wreck, not realizing how badly I was hurt, and desperately searched for the other car. I saw it resting nearby in a parking lot, surrounded by chunks of metal and bits of windshield. It was half its original size and leaned oddly on its right wheels. No sign of Thomas. The rain felt like needles poking me. "He couldn't have survived," I thought. If he did, I could only imagine how badly his legs would be crushed beneath the dashboard, and for some reason, I felt that he would never play football again. Mount de Sales had lost its chance to win the state championship a few weeks before. "Maybe next year," I had told my brother. What if there was going to be no next year now?

But before the scream could escape my throat, the door of the car cracked open and a tall, black figure stepped out, un-touched and unhurt. The needles poked me harder to shake my disbelief, and this time the rain poured in happiness. I fell to the ground, marveling at a miracle.

Thomas ran to my side, leaned over me, and took me in his arms so that the worry needles found their mark on his back. No one had stopped to help us, but like a faithful friend, he assured me that I would be safe. A salty taste filled my mouth, and though I dozed off with the notion that it was my own blood, I hadn't realized my brother's tears were falling on my face.

Everyone would cry the night I dreamed we won the big game.

It had been five weeks since the accident and my neck still hurt. I saw the hulking figures on the football field and cringed at the bodily collisions that sounded out every play. The players reminded me of huge automobiles bumping each other hard and causing multiple pileups. My accident kept replaying before my eyes. I knew we needed another miracle. I also worried for number 72.

That was near the end of the third quarter, and with a touchdown that gave us a one-point lead came hope. Bent forward on the edge of my seat, I squinted to find my brother who had just emerged from the bottom of a tackle. He raised his arms to rally the crowd and to inspire whatever hope they'd lacked before.

The pileups seemed different to me now. My brother had not only been there for me like a best friend, but he was also there for his team and their fans, like everyone's friend. I no longer heard clashing metal and breaking glass in my head. Instead, I delighted in the memory of the strong, agile legs of a wonderful defensive guard rushing to help me out of the rain. His actions then had saved my life. Now they had turned the game around. They had made miracles commonplace. Three seconds . . . two . . . one! And there was glory.

I woke up and smiled happily. "Maybe next year," I thought.

Craig Reynolds
Holy Cross High School
Louisville, Kentucky

Karen M. Lewis
Central Catholic
High School
Lafayette, Indiana

Stories That Bind Us

Should I knock on the door? Well, probably not. She might get mad. I don't think she likes to be bothered. I'll just leave. I'm sure she doesn't want my company. These were the thoughts that first passed through my mind when I met Emma.

I would only see her occasionally when she came out to yell at the neighborhood kids to stay out of her driveway. Then she would go back inside until she felt it was time to yell at them again. I used to feel inclined to believe my younger brother, who claimed that she liked to eat little kids.

This was my perception of her for about two years. Only within the past two weeks has this image slowly started to break down. I still see a person who isn't particularly fond of children, but now I understand why. She is older and can no longer deal with the youthfulness of children. However, she is still filled with life herself.

She is constantly traveling from one place to another. This week she is leaving for Washington D.C., and she has another trip planned upon her return. She always asks me before she leaves if I can "care for her babies." No, at the age of sixty, she doesn't have little children. Her babies are Abbie, her dog, and Chrissy, her cat.

Abbie is a golden retriever, which has special meaning for her because she has had seven dogs of this breed over the years. Each recalls a special story.

Emma had her first, very special golden retriever for nearly seventeen years. Just yesterday she was showing me pictures of him, and she told me about the day before they had to have him put to sleep. This was years ago, but I could still see the pain in her eyes and hear her voice begin to crack as she told me the story. They had a pizza party at her house that day so the dog could have a pleasant evening before he was put to sleep. She spent all night comforting him to sleep. The following morning she called the doctor. He suggested that he come get the dog from her and put him down at his house, but she refused his offer. She said, "My dog has lived all his life here, and I'm not going to send him away to die." She then held his head as the doctor gave him the injection and held him until he was gone. They buried him under the grapevine where he always liked to play.

This is the way I now see Emma. She is a person who loves animals just as much as I do. We share a feeling that animals are just like people and have the same thoughts, feelings, and love to share that the rest of us do.

Emma is becoming closer to me as I find out more about her. She has lived through times that I have only read about. She knows the feelings of V-J Day and has experienced everything that goes with war. She entered the United States Army Nursing Corps after receiving a letter in the mail giving her the choice to either be drafted or to enlist. She enlisted and was sent to France. After only a short time, she was celebrating the Allied Forces' victory in Europe. A few months later, her ship, the *Monterey*, sailed to the Philippines. The very day that they arrived in Manila Harbor, the Japanese surrendered to the United States. In a newspaper article covering V-J Day, she was quoted saying laughingly: "When I got to France, the Germans surrendered, and then I got to the Philippines and the Japanese surrendered. They must have known I was coming."

This was a great day for the troops. Everyone was jumping up and down in excitement. The war was finally over, and they were going home. Emma, however, didn't make it back to her home state of New Jersey, but instead came to Indiana. After coming home from the Pacific, she went on a blind date and ended up marrying him. They both moved to Indiana where her husband had a job offer. However, she says that she received a special sign on V-J Day that told her she was going back to New Jersey sometime. While they were celebrating, the battleship *New Jersey* pulled up next to them. She said that she knew then that she was definitely going home.

This young girl is the person I now see when I look at her. She has experienced many things in life that I may never see, but I now realize that this doesn't make her old. It just makes her more of a person. She is a spirited woman who loves to share her past with others, especially people my age.

All this time I didn't think she would even want to hear my voice, but now I can see that she enjoys each time that we recall the events of the past together. She's proud of it, and just needs someone to show interest. It seems that over the years her joy of being an army nurse had been forgotten by all others, but not by her. She will always remember the day that the USS *New Jersey* pulled up beside her, and they looked at it in wonder, realizing that they appeared no bigger than a rowboat beside it.

In the past few weeks, I have learned more about her than I had ever known in the two years before. Each evening I go to her house to get the paper, and while I am there she shares her story with me.

She may be older than my other friends, but she can give me something that they cannot. Through her, I can see the past, and I hope that I am giving her a vision of the future.

K. S. C.
Ursuline Academy of
Cincinnati
Cincinnati, Ohio

Same Here

"I love you, but I just don't know if I'm *in* love with you."

As the words stumbled from my quivering lips, I finally forced my averted eyes to abandon their study of the floor and instead to focus on him to whom I spoke. But, with relief, I realized that his eyes were having as much difficulty concentrating on me as mine were on him. I knew that they would.

He sat on my couch, chocolate eyes staring straight ahead of him, too tense to change his gaze. It was as if he sought some refuge in the dark window across the room, for he eyed its blackness with such pleading and vulnerability that he appeared to be a lost little child, not a seventeen-year-old boy. His movements, too, suggested hints of childhood. He squirmed in his seat, fidgety and flustered, pretending that he was merely *physically* uncomfortable, when really it was his emotions that were ill at ease. His awkwardness was so apparent, as much as he tried to disguise it, that it made me return my own gaze to the safety of the floor. Neither one of us was very good at this.

He quickly cleared his throat to break the silence, though it was obvious that this was its only purpose. His throat could not have been tired; he had not uttered a single word the entire time that I had spilled my guts. But then again, I had not expected him to. He wouldn't do that.

My eyes, still glued to the carpet, were suddenly attracted to a movement in my periphery. I realized that his foot was shaking. I could tell that the motion of this twitching brown hiking boot was a mirror of his churning insides. Not only was his shoe atremble, but also his entire jean-clad left leg. As my eyes followed the shiver, I realized that it did not end there. The anxiety had spread all the way to his soft fingertips dangling precariously at his mouth. They were in grave danger of being chewed, as usual. I wanted to reach out and hold this tender hand, so often abused by worry, but I was as uncomfortable as he was. I too was held fast in my place. It was a wonder that we ever moved.

But just when I thought that my attempt at openness would go unanswered, I lifted my head at the sound of a sniffle. Again I dared to search for his searching eyes, and this time I found them looking back at me. Milky now with watery tears, his deep brown eyes stared into my own and told me all I ever needed to know. His lips began to tremble as he opened his mouth to give a silent whisper, too quiet to be heard, yet too loud to be forgotten, and though I never heard the words, I saw them in his face. "Same here," shone his eyes, dripped his tears, glowed his cheeks. "Same here," curled his hair, shook his chin. "Same here," licked his lips, bit his teeth, scrunched his nose. "Same here," and at that, we were friends.

Name Withheld
The Academy of
Saint Elizabeth
Convent Station, New Jersey

Taking a Major Chance

Friendship? What exactly is friendship? I never understood the concept of it. I often asked my friends how they defined it. They would say, "It is a confidant, someone you trust, someone who is there in both good and bad times." My mother told me, "By the time you graduate high school, you will be able to count all your real friends on one hand." How depressing! I wanted more than five friends. What could she have possibly meant by that? Tiphani answered that for me.

I have been friends with Tiphani since we were both three years old. Tiphani is different. I guess you could say she's had her share of hard times. Her father died of heart failure two days before Christmas when she was a little girl. Tiphani was devastated. Things were never the same after that. Tiphani and her mother could find no common ground. By the time we were twelve, she was severely depressed. Tiphani blamed her mother for her father's death. She always felt desperate and trapped without him. She despised her mother.

Then, during the summer a few years ago, I was going to her house. I could see police lights, and a horrible feeling curdled my stomach. I knew it was Tiphani. She was standing on the edge of her roof, threatening to jump.

No one saw me go into the house. I went to the window and screamed, "Tiphani!" She came inside and curled up in a ball on the floor. All I could do was hold her. I could not tell her it would be okay because I knew it wouldn't be. She ended up in a psychiatric hospital. For the next three years, she was in and out of hospitals and residential programs.

Everyone said therapy would help her. I saw the real Tiphani. She was more lost and lonely than ever. She tried to fill the empty spot in her heart with drugs and sex. When she finally came home for good after three years of treatment, she was not the same. I was actually scared of her. We never talked about anything that bothered her. Sometimes she would come to my house, lay on the floor, and cry for hours. I never said much. I don't think she wanted me to. The important thing was that she knew I was there for her.

Finally, on Christmas a year later, I realized what friendship was. I am not Catholic, but every Christmas Eve I go to midnight Mass. Tiphani asked if she could go with me. I was shocked. Tiphani had not celebrated Christmas since the day her father died. I felt honored to have her go with me.

The church was beautiful with all the lights and singing. I felt warmly peaceful. The priest spoke about friendship and hope. He said that friendship and love are like taking a major chance. You give your all and hope it's worth it. That is what God did when he gave us Jesus. The choir sang "When Christ Was Born." I started crying. I looked at Tiphani and she was also crying. She hugged me, something we had never done in our entire lives.

After Mass, Tiphani went to the priest and thanked him for the beautiful sermon. At that very moment, she saw just as much joy and hope in the world as I did. I knew right then and there that my friendship with Tiphani was worth it. We could withstand anything together.

Joseph Emmons
Saint Viator High School
Arlington Heights, Illinois

Semantha Dena
Father Yermo High School
El Paso, Texas

I Forgive You

The last talk I had with Giovanni was terrible because we had a fight. It happened like this.

As my boyfriend was leaving my house, Giovanni came in and surprised us. They stared at each other. After a while, Giovanni turned and walked into my room. My boyfriend left and I went to my room to speak to Giovanni.

Giovanni looked at me for a while and finally said, "What the hell are you doing with that piece of crap?"

"Why is he a piece of crap?"

With a surprised face, he said: "You call yourself my best friend? Don't you remember? He's the guy who took Katrina away from me, the only person I really cared about except for you."

"How was I supposed to know he was that guy?"

"By his name, you idiot!" he hollered.

Tears came to my eyes. "I forgot, I'm sorry."

I guess he felt sorry too because he said: "Look, I forgive you. I know you'll break up with him."

I looked at him with disbelief. "But he cares about me."

"Semantha," he said with anger, "I don't want you to break up with him because I hate him. He told Katrina he cared about her, too. Then a month later she came back to me saying that he went out on her."

I did not believe him. "You're lying, you just hate him. You still care about Katrina and you are still hurt, so you want us to break up. You don't want me to be happy unless you are happy." He tried to say something, but I did not let him. "Leave, I don't want to see your face."

He turned and left, though something inside of me did not want him to go. But I was hurt, and my pride was not going to be broken. A week after this, I broke up with my boyfriend. Giovanni had been right.

About two weeks later, I received a letter from Giovanni's mother. When I first saw it, I wondered why his mom would write to me. As soon as I opened it, I got a sick feeling. I saw tear spots on the paper.

The letter began innocently enough with questions about my family. Then she wrote, "But I have some bad news." As soon as I read that, I began to cry. I did not want to read on because the night before I had dreamt that I had walked up to a coffin and looked in. It was Giovanni. I woke up and cried for the rest of the night.

Now, because of the dream, I was afraid to continue reading. My mom walked in and sat next to me, and I asked her to read the rest of the letter. Giovanni had been out with some friends, walking along some street at about nine o'clock at night. All of a sudden, some guys came out of a house yelling stuff. One of them took out a gun and fired three shots. One of those shots hit Giovanni in the neck. He could hardly speak and was still in critical condition. She wrote that he was heavily sedated and hardly ever awake because of the constant pain. When awake, he asked for me. She wanted me to fly to California.

As soon as my mother finished reading me the letter, she made a reservation for me. I went to California by myself. I wanted to get my thoughts together before I got to the hospital so that Giovanni would think nothing was wrong.

Giovanni's mom was a wreck. His family told me that she had not been home since he was shot. They said that she wanted to see me with him before she would leave. Before I went in to see him, I told her to go home and sleep. It took me awhile to convince her to go, but I managed it. I then walked into the intensive care unit and asked the nurse what curtain Giovanni was behind. I started toward it, but stopped. I was afraid of what I might see, but something pushed me to open the curtain.

Giovanni was asleep, so I sat down in a chair next to him. I was there for two of the longest hours of my life. Then he finally woke up and saw me. His eyes lit up. He pointed to a notepad on the table. I handed it to him along with a pen. He started writing. It took him a while.

When he handed the notepad back to me, it read: "Is this the only way I can get you to come see me? Don't worry, I don't care. I'm glad you came. I want you to do something for me. I want you to go out and buy a birthday card and a Mother's Day card for my mom. Don't ask me why, just go, and don't tell anyone. Go now." I turned to him and smiled, then I left. I went down to the gift shop at the hospital, got the best cards, and returned.

I walked in. He was still awake. I handed him the cards, and he started writing in them. When he finished, he closed the cards and handed them to me. I put them in my bag and then he started writing to me on the notepad. "I'm going to die very soon. On my mom's birthday and on Mother's Day, I want you to send those cards to her. I don't want you to be sad. I need you to help my mom get through this. You are my best friend, and I want to thank you for everything you have done and for what you will continue to do. I want you to make sure that the people who did this to me are put in jail. Tell my mom that I will be happy in heaven. My dad came down from heaven to tell me that I will be happy. Tell her that we love her and will miss her. I love you too, Semantha, and I will miss you too. I will always be with you. Don't ever forget me."

When I finished reading the letter, I turned to look at him. He smiled at me and closed his eyes. With his eyes closed, he managed to say, "I forgive you." Giovanni died an hour later. I lost my best friend, and I did not get to say anything to him.

It took some time for the police to find the people who killed my friend. It took a lot more time for court proceedings to go through. I had to speak to the judge about Giovanni. I had to tell him what kind of person he was. The newspapers had said that Giovanni was in a rival gang, so I had to tell the judge that they were wrong. The killers are now serving twenty-five years in prison. They are eligible for parole in eleven years. I will do my best to keep them in jail for the whole twenty-five years.

Ben Collinger
Marist School
Atlanta, Georgia

One Close Friend

Being a good friend and having a good friend have always been very important to me. I would rather have one close friend that I can count on than ten friends that would be fair-weather friends. Neither race, nationality, nor religion have ever been a factor in judging or choosing my friends.

One incident that I remember the most, happened when I was in fourth grade. My friend Michael and I had been best friends since we were in kindergarten. Michael was often teased, called names, and made fun of, and I never understood why until I got older. Michael was the only black kid in our class. He was disliked just because his skin was a different color.

One morning during math class, the teacher falsely accused Michael of disrupting the class. One of the other students had thrown a spitball across the room and accidentally hit her. She immediately blamed Michael and gave him a Friday detention. I told her he didn't do it, but she would not believe me. I hated to see him being punished for something he didn't do. So at nine years old, I went to the principal's office to defend my friend. I was scared to death because, basically, I was very shy. She listened carefully, and thanked me for coming to see her. She spoke to the teacher and, as a result, found the kid who actually threw the spitball.

Michael and I are still great friends and will always be there for each other.

Katheryn Patterson
Schools of the
Sacred Heart
San Francisco, California

Waiting for the Sun

A thick silence enshrouds the dark house, and noises, normally hidden behind voices and everyday clatter, shyly cry out to the night. A thin sliver of light escapes from under my partially closed door and it guides me from the kitchen, through the blind hallway, to my waiting textbook. I plop myself heavily on the hard wooden chair that sits in front of my desk and grudgingly thumb the pages till I get to the Revolutionary War, tomorrow's exam material. I know I should have started studying earlier, but I had to watch *Party of Five*, and I had promised Stan I would call him. Wishing I didn't have history first period the next day, I begin to read the microscopic print.

Time seems to fly by and leave me behind. Through my window I think I can see soft daylight spilling over the horizon, but I know it's just my sleepy eyes telling me it's time for bed. A shrill ringing assaults my ears. It seems to come from somewhere in the house, but I decide to drown out my body's signs of fatigue with a soft, cushy set of earphones. It isn't until Alanis launches into her hit song and Paul Revere alerts the troops that I realize it's the doorbell echoing through the sleeping house.

Amazed that anyone would be here at this hour, I pull the door open without asking who it is. I blink my eyes several times before they adjust to the porch light. Finally, I am able to see the intruder.

104

"Megan, what are you doing here? What's wrong?" Her large brown eyes are swollen shut, her rose-colored cheeks stained a dismal shade of red. Her lower lip begins to tremble as she tries in vain to hold back the tears. I rush forward and wrap my arms around her normally solid, now fragile, figure. Her body convulses against mine as huge sobs bubble up from deep within her. Never letting go of her, I lead her into my room, not caring if we wake my mother. I sit with her on my bed, and she cries in my arms for what seems like an eternity. Finally she pulls away and looks at me with weepy eyes.

"My parents are getting divorced," she whispers, her voice barely audible. "I just found out. I came down here as soon as they told me. I had to get away from there. Kat, what am I going to do? How could they . . ." Her voice had risen several octaves before drowning in a fresh flood of tears.

My concern for tomorrow's exam melts and disappears while I listen to my best friend's shaky voice telling me about her family problems. Knowing neither of us will sleep tonight, we sip hot chocolate in the dark and wait for the sun to come up.

Friendship Is Forever

Susan Eylward
Bishop Kearney High School
Brooklyn, New York

Friend must be the hardest word to define. It entails much more than the simple one-word definitions, "a companion" or "an acquaintance," given by some dictionaries. To me a friend is the one who shares your laughter and your secrets, a rock to lean on during rough times, your private comedian who brings a smile to your face when you are down, and a spirit similar to your own that understands you like no one else could. A friend is like your diary, one who lacks judgment and criticism, one who knows all your feelings and thoughts, and one whom you can trust.

When I was nine years old, my best friend, Erin, moved away. I cried for weeks and nothing could console me. My father told me, "Friends may come and go, but family is forever." Somehow I just couldn't accept that statement.

Erin and I had done everything together. When we were two, we made mud pies together in my backyard. When we were five, we discovered how much fun it was to bother our older sisters. When we were seven, we learned to ride our bikes. When we were eight, we crossed the street for the first time without adult supervision.

Being without my best friend at the age of nine was extremely upsetting. It meant living without the only person who understood as well as I did that Barbie could not wear her pink blouse with her red skirt. It meant living without the only person who also thought going to the supermarket was a game we played, rather than a chore. It meant living without the only person who knew all my childhood dreams, wishes, and secrets and accepted them as realistic.

It took me a while to realize that Erin really was not coming back. Eventually I started staying with other children, and soon I had a new best friend. Erin and I tried to keep in touch, but we lost contact. After a while it didn't even matter that much to me.

Considering all this, you can imagine my shock when my doorbell rang last summer and I found Erin standing outside my house. We stared at each other for a couple of minutes, not knowing what to say. She looked different, to say the least. Even though I had grown up, I never pictured her to be more than nine years old. It was awkward, standing there lost between the past and the present, trying to figure out where we fit in. Then she smiled, and in a familiar voice called me by a childhood name I had not heard for years. With that simple greeting I looked at her, and I could almost see the nine-year-old girl.

Erin had only come back for a visit to see the old neighborhood. We stayed up late, sitting on my stoop and talking. We reminisced about almost-forgotten memories, and we laughed about old jokes. As we sat there, licking our Italian ices from the corner pizza parlor, wearing our hair in ponytails, telling each other secrets, I felt as if I was a child again, and I realized friendship really does last forever.

I talk to Erin regularly now, and she is one of my good friends. I discovered that a friend does not have to be someone right across the street all the time, but someone who is there for you all the time. So the other day, when my dad was repeating his favorite saying, I told him that I had come up with my own. Upon his questioning, I told him, "Time may come and go, but friendship is forever."

Mandi Lin Gacioch
De La Salle High School
Minneapolis, Minnesota

BFF, Best Friends Forever

In about the seventh grade, I started to go through many changes with my friends. I began to see my life differently and more seriously. I started to hang around with a couple of new friends, especially a girl named Katie. As time went on, our friendship grew to be something more meaningful. We began sleeping over at each other's house, getting to know each other's family, enjoying each other's company, and considering each other BFF, Best Friends Forever. Her home was like my second home, and her mom, Laurie, like my second mom.

Laurie, however, was very ill. She had had heart problems since age fourteen. Katie was a miracle child because of this. Laurie was constantly in congestive heart failure and in the hospital. Year before last, she was put in the hospital twice in one month. I visited her at the hospital all the time. Laurie was getting to the point where she couldn't recognize people or talk very sensibly. I could see how much this hurt Katie, and I wished she would talk to me, but I didn't want to pry.

Finally, Laurie had surgery. Odds were only fifty-fifty of her making it through. With the power of prayers answered, she did. Then Laurie's health went up and down for a whole month. When she remained in ICU for so long, people seemed to be giving up hope. This made me angry because I felt that if they gave up hope, Laurie might too. I, for one, couldn't give up hope. Katie's and my friendship began to grow. We talked more, trusted more, and felt each other's pain.

About a month after Laurie's surgery, my mom woke me up with a look on her face that I will never forget. She told me that Laurie wasn't going to make it through the hour. She told me that Katie's Uncle Timmy called and wanted me to come to the hospital to help Katie. I tried to wake myself up from the horrible nightmare, but I couldn't. In a strange state of shock, I got up, dressed, and went to the hospital.

My parents and I arrived at the hospital just when Laurie died. That's when I heard Katie screaming frantically and saying things that crushed my heart. I was trying to stay strong for her, but I couldn't. I was looking for the same look as she was, the look that said everything was going to be all right. I couldn't find it and she couldn't either.

I went home, feeling like there was nothing I could do for Katie. I went home to sleep for an hour or so, but I couldn't. Later, I went to her house. There was nothing I could say or do to make her feel any better.

A year later, Katie's and my friendship is extremely strong. We can confide completely in each other. She told me later that I was the first person she saw at the hospital. I felt that she knew I was there for her and always would be. This made me glad.

This friendship that I have found is one I will never lose. Katie is a huge part of my life. I would feel empty without her in my life. We have proven that we will be there for each other, that we can trust each other, and that God has made us such good friends. We are BFF, Best Friends Forever.

Richard J. Linden
Bishop Chatard High School
Indianapolis, Indiana

Déjà Vu

In Indiana, the month of March means one thing—basketball. The annual NCAA national tournament had begun, and my father and I anxiously sat down to watch our Purdue Boilermakers take on an underdog team. Purdue had been placed in the Midwest Regional, and it just so happened that the site for the opening two rounds was the Hoosier Dome. Therefore, Purdue was going to have the advantage of playing in front of a hometown crowd.

As the player and coach introductions were taking place, I glanced at my father and saw a look of complete shock on his previously mild-mannered face. Before I had time to question him about it, he had already begun to wildly shout, "That's Mike!" Once again, before I could ask who "Mike" was, he leapt from his chair and rushed into the kitchen to get my mother's attention. After both of my parents had calmed down, they explained the reason for their spontaneous excitement.

The underdog opponent that Purdue was playing was Northeast Louisiana University. When their head coach, Mike Vining, was introduced, my father recognized a face and a name that he had neither seen nor spoken to in the past twenty years. My father went on to explain that during his nine-month tour in Vietnam, his closest friend had been a tall, thin, basketball nut from Louisiana named Mike Vining. The last time he had spoken to Mike was the day he left Vietnam to return home to my mother and sister. As he told me this story, I couldn't help but notice the tears that were forming in his reminiscing eyes.

After the initial shock had worn off, we embarked on a frenzy of phone calls to local hotels in an attempt to locate where Mike's team was staying. With no luck, but a determination that I had never before seen in my father, we traveled to the airport on Saturday morning in an attempt to catch the team before their plane headed back to Louisiana.

We parked the car, and entered the USAir terminal. The first person I laid eyes on was a member of the Northeast Louisiana basketball team. Before I could tell my dad, he was walking over to talk to his once best friend. When he put his hand on Mike's arm to get his attention, the reaction I saw from Mike was one of *déjà vu*. He had been talking with another coach, and amazedly smiled and said, "I don't believe it, Lucky Linden."

Although Mike had an entire team to get on a plane in less than half an hour, the three of us sat down and they began to catch up on the past twenty years. In the exchange that was to take place over the next thirteen minutes, I would learn more about friendships than I had in the previous thirteen years. I was awestruck by the sense of camaraderie and brotherhood that I felt at the restaurant table on that Saturday morning.

I began to grow a little confused as I realized that I apparently still had a lot to learn. At that point, it seemed there was only one thing I could remain fairly certain about. I knew that my father and Mike Vining would never lose touch again.

Bridget Venckus
Saint Vincent High School
Petaluma, California

Why I Was Talkin' to Her

I met Hilary in my eighth-grade year of junior high. She was in the seventh grade and was your average junior high outcast. She was short and very overweight, wore thick, Coke bottle glasses, and had hair that was bright orange after a failed attempt to dye it. Hilary had physical education (PE) at the same time I did, and I remember people calling her names or quietly talking and pointing out how big she was when she could barely do her exercises.

At first, I didn't think much about this funny-looking girl, who was constantly made fun of, except that maybe I felt a little sorry for her. I was the big eighth grader. What did I care about this girl? I had no idea that this little girl with orange hair and thick glasses would help me change the way I looked at the world.

PE was not the only class I had with Hilary. Although I was in eighth grade, I had to take a seventh-grade Spanish class, and she was in it. I was perfectly okay with this because there were other eighth graders in the class, so we basically went about ignoring the seventh graders.

Hilary sat next to my friend Sharon. Sharon didn't like this very much because she thought Hilary was annoying. You see, because Hilary had been made fun of for so long, she had absolutely no confidence in herself, let alone in her ability to speak another language. Every time the teacher would call on

Hilary, she could not answer. Then Hilary would get very upset because the other kids would laugh at her more. As time went on, Hilary would cry silently behind her thick glasses, and I saw that she needed a friend. I told Sharon I would switch seats with her, and I would sit next to Hilary.

At first, I think Hilary wasn't sure if she could trust me. But I think she hungered for a friend, and I was the only one around who was willing to be that person. I tried to help Hilary the best I could with Spanish, but she was not doing work in her other classes either. I knew she could do the work and I hated to see her fail, so I became her all-around tutor. Hilary would tell me about her assignments and I would nag her sometimes like a mother, to be sure she got them done.

I didn't know much about Hilary's mom, but I knew she worked long hours and wasn't around to help Hilary much. I remember Hilary telling me about her dad. Once she said he had some problems but he was trying to change his ways, and I was sorry and scared for her. Hilary lived in a small shack of a house, but she never seemed to complain. I began to see how lucky I was.

I continued to help Hilary throughout the school year, and I think she started to improve. Hilary was a good person, but no one knew it except me. People would come up to me and ask why I was talking to *her* and all I could say was because she was my friend. They would usually walk away with a disgusted look on their face, but they didn't understand, they couldn't! If they would just take the time to get to know the people who aren't so cool or beautiful, they would see that those people can be caring, kind, and considerate. At Christmastime Hilary gave me a gift, a small bracelet that was made out of tin. It wasn't expensive, but it was all she had to give.

Eighth grade went by quickly, and I graduated from junior high praying that Hilary would make it through the eighth grade okay. When I graduated, I not only took with me all the new knowledge I had gained, but I had also gained a new friend. Hilary taught me that to know someone for who they truly are as a human being, you have to look beyond the fact that they are overweight or not cool, and understand that they have feelings and are hurt when they are made fun of. I also learned to appreciate everything I have.

Hilary has called me once or twice since I started high school, telling me about her awful schedule and mean teachers, but when I ask her if she's happy, she pauses for a minute and says, "Yes."

Jeff Markwardt
Shanley High School
Fargo, North Dakota

Michael J. Pugliese
Lancaster Catholic
High School
Lancaster, Pennsylvania

Big-Time Support

After ten weeks of intensive practice and eight games, Peter had only collected a few minutes of varsity action. Even though his senior year season had already started, Peter still stood a few inches closer to the grass than the rest of the players and had to wrap his uniform belt around his waist a bit more than one and a half times to prevent embarrassment. He had worked hard for four years, doing everything his coaches asked of him. What he had in desire, he lacked in talent and confidence.

Each practice Peter pushed himself to improve and tried to prove himself. Despite some minor improvements, he never got any higher on the depth chart than third string.

At every game, he stood on the sidelines in his immaculate, full uniform, helmet on, chin strap buttoned, and mouthpiece ready to go. Even so, he accepted his position on the sideline and would scream for all the guys that were in the game. He never stopped hoping that he might get in and never stopped screaming for his teammates. Peter's teammate, Jim, a fearsome starter who appeared twice Peter's size, constantly encouraged him to keep dreaming while always exaggerating Peter's contribution to the team. "All I could hear out there was that little squeaky voice cheering us on," Big Jim would always tell Peter.

Every player on the team tried to build Peter's confidence, while constantly showing him respect. They never played any pranks on him. They never ragged him for mistakes. They

116

constantly offered advice and little hints on just how to position the hands or just when to make the cut.

A few of the players that weighed almost twice Peter's weight offered him a different sign of respect. Peter would often volunteer to be part of the scout or practice defense. This required nothing more than pretending to be a member of the opposing team, and then allowing his own teammates to practice their moves on him. Despite Peter's continual invitation to do their best and not to worry about hurting him, his powerful teammates, including Big Jim, would often rush at him, smile, and unnoticeably to the coaches, ease up before contact.

After three years and seven and three-quarters games of his senior year, closing minutes of the last game saw Peter cheering his team from the sidelines as they coasted along on a fourteen point lead. Head Coach Morris was entering substitute players. Peter got close but stopped short of the coach, knowing that more talented players were also crowding the coach for an opportunity to play.

Big Jim knew that Peter wouldn't push his way to the front of the crowd of substitutes. So, when Coach Morris demanded more substitutes, Big Jim quickly reached down, grabbed Peter, and pushed him right into the bellowing coach. Then he yelled, "Hey, Coach, Peter hasn't been in yet."

Coach Morris scowled at Peter, and then jerked him onto the field. Surprised and extremely nervous, the little backup ran onto the field for some of his own action. Big Jim stood on the sidelines, cheering mightily for Peter.

Although Peter didn't make any special blocks, tackles, catches, or anything else noteworthy, Peter found Big Jim and a circle of his friends waiting on the sidelines to congratulate him.

Irene Sola'nge McCalphin
Xavier Preparatory School
New Orleans, Louisiana

Diamonds

"I can't wait. After nine years it is finally over. Freedom! Sweet freedom!" Raymond shouted, almost colliding with me as he ran up the steps of the Saint Anthony of Padua church. I glanced at him sharply. "Come on, Irene, you've been here as long as I have. I know that you're jumping for joy." He put an arm around my shoulders and smiled. His whole face lit up under his mass of straight, light brown hair. Red flushed into his cheeks and his green eyes sparkled. "I forgot how hard you cried yesterday. Still a little sentimental, huh? It's not in your nature to cry."

I tried to walk away from him, but he had his arm securely around my shoulders and every step I took, he took with me. I was embarrassed enough without his teasing. Yesterday our class had rehearsals for graduation, and I ended up crying so uncontrollably that even he was moved to sympathize.

That night I called another friend on the phone and ended up crying again. After I stopped crying and she was sure that I was all right, she began fussing about how everyone had called her and done the same thing and how if she could have gotten through the phone line she would have slapped every one of them. I can't say I was shocked about it, Jackie was always on the rough side.

I snapped back to the present when Raymond tore away and began running after the other boys on their way home. Regretfully they all stopped, and Aquiles shouted, "Hurry up,

Medusa, before we leave you." He liked to make fun of my hair, which I wore in braids. I tried not to blush at his words, but even through my dark skin it showed.

For the last two years, I was the only girl in an all-boy group that walked home from school together. I had to listen to all their pickup lines and the gory details of fights and movies. Sometimes they would stop halfway home to play football, and I had to wait until they finished. Today I was sure they were going to play with my nerves instead of the football.

Before I reached them, I heard fake sobbing. And when I caught up to them, the sobs got louder. I felt sure that I would never miss them. For the remainder of the walk, which took five minutes but seemed like thirty, I promised myself that I would not cry again until after graduation tomorrow night. I only had a few hours to go.

Before we processed in for the ceremony, some of the boys made a bet on who would cry first. Needless to say, they all had their money on me.

During the ceremony I looked around at some of my friends. Elizabeth, with her long, red hair and green eyes, who pushed me to do my best no matter what. Marcelo, who had the dark hair that I always wanted to play in. He was always there to give me good advice, even though half the time he didn't realize what he was saying. And Thanh, with her slanted, dark, mischievous eyes that always saw my mistakes and made sure that I would never forget them. I could hardly believe that all the years had gone by so quickly. All the jokes and tears, all the fights and make ups. We tried to get away with some of the craziest things, and often did.

One by one a name was called, one by one someone that I held dear was gone. One by one we would set out on whatever path God led us on, even though it now meant traveling alone.

Friends are like newly found diamonds covered in dirt and coal. You will never know their beauty until you have chipped away the cover with tools of love and understanding. Inside, something wonderful but different awaits. Each possesses a love that can cut through fear, racism, and pain with a light so brilliant that it is not limited to only one color but includes the entire spectrum. And I can say with a good heart that I am rich beyond imagination.

Laura Lawless
Dominican Academy
New York, New York

Da

One year ago, I lost the greatest friend I've ever known. This friend was my grandfather, but to me he was always "Da." There were no pretenses or formalities. We were just best friends.

The morning started as many others had for the past few months. Being a leisurely Sunday morning, warm for a winter day, I decided to stay in bed as long as possible. Having exhausted excuses for not getting up, I reluctantly stretched my legs and proceeded to raid the refrigerator, looking for bacon, eggs, toast, and jam—the kind of breakfast that's only excusable on Sundays. There was no bacon and my grandmother was saving the eggs for a cake, so I hesitantly prepared a stale bagel. Unsatisfied, I walked into the living room that had been converted into a quasi-infirmary, complete with all the modern amenities of many hospital rooms.

Da was sleeping lightly in his bed by the television set. Naturally this annoyed me, because I couldn't turn it on yet. Immediately I regretted thinking this, because my complaints couldn't begin to compare with the pain he was feeling. He had terminal cancer, and the suffering was unbearable, even for him.

I sat in the folding chair by his bed and looked at his sleeping body. I stared at his closed eyes and remembered when blindness had not taken his sight and he could use those eyes to read and explore and to see me. For four years he couldn't even recognize his best friend. I wondered what he saw now as he slept. Was he dreaming? Was he completely aware? The night before, he hadn't made much sense. I hoped that this effect of the medicine would end soon. His eyes spoke louder than words. The test of true friendship is the ability to read another's eyes. His were a light hazel, constantly in motion. Even when he claimed to feel fine, his eyes still revealed the truth. I loved his eyes, and I missed being able to see my reflection in them. I wondered if he knew what I looked like. How many other people have friends as devoted as he was? He loved without seeing and trusted without proof, gave without reluctance and cared without recompense. And he was *my* best friend.

Next, I stared at his hands. They looked so different now. The cancer had depleted him, and his once firm hands were now transparent and thin. I slipped my hand into his as I had so many times before, but now it was limp and unresponsive. I have many pictures of him holding me as a baby with his hands wrapped tightly around me, protective and sheltering. Now they lay motionless. I could feel his pulse beating slowly. How many other people had a friend who had love flowing through his or her veins? How many people were loved by a friend who would lay down his or her life without a moment's pause? How many others were as blessed as I was to know a person who had such a deep concern for others? and to be their best friend?

The hands that had guided and protected now were tired and old. Age and sickness had stolen my best friend and left in his place a weak shadow of his former self. The eyes that glimmered with hope for my future and that of his whole family were now closed gently. Even in that state, he knew me and squeezed my hand affectionately, assuring me one last time that I was not just a relative but an intimate friend of his.

I felt that the time was drawing near for God to take his hand, not me, and lead him back to heaven. He opened his eyes, and I promised him I would be back soon, right after I showered and changed out of my pajamas. He smiled, and I kissed his forehead, telling him that I would see him in a minute. When I returned, hair wet and clothes mismatched, the hand that I had held moments ago had dropped to his side and his eyes were no longer strained in the grip of pain. I knew without shock or surprise that my closest friend was with God now. No one could deserve it more.

I kissed his forehead once again and stepped back to see the hands, eyes, and heart of a best friend, my best friend. I promised him I would see him again soon and, God willing, in time I will. Until then, I know that God will take good care of his spirit. God is the only one I would trust my best friend with.

Melissa Ann Wood
Nerinx Hall
Webster Groves, Missouri

Angels

Friends are the mirrors that allow us to see our true beauty. I have two types of friends, my companions and my angels. My companions are the beautiful people who share their life with me; my angels are the people who show me God's magic. Let me tell you about some of my angels.

My grandmother was an angel—beautiful in the light and radiant in the dark. She blessed everything she saw, and saw everything as blessed. I'd like to believe that one day I will be as unselfish as she was, that love will come as easily to me as it did to her, and that the words "I love you" will be more familiar to me. She lived her life in God's footsteps and held God's hand. When she touched me I could feel how much she loved me, and her words, they were always true. I often wonder why I didn't tell her this, but I believe she listens now. When she died, I understood why, yet words cannot explain. I miss her, and I often wish I could just have one last conversation with her. Ah, the things I would say.

But I can almost feel her eyes on these words, and she's smiling. My memories of my grandmother keep her alive, so everyday I remember her. I remember how she was always busy making everyone else happy. I remember how she would let me help her cook, even though I did everything wrong. I remember that she told me I was beautiful. I remember how she would tell me stories, and I remember her singing at church. I remember her love.

I did not cry at her funeral, and when I placed the rose on her grave, I did not weep. But when I sat at the kitchen table in her house and rubbed my hands over the wood, remembering how many times her hands had rested on the table, then I cried. And when I saw that all the flowers she had planted had died, then I wept. Now she is in my heart. Now she is a piece of my soul. My grandmother is an angel.

Below him, an orange plastic tray with his dinner; above him, a ray of light. I go to school to learn math from a teacher who has a degree in education, but I go to a homeless shelter to learn about faith from a man who has a degree in life. He told me of his night of being left alone, he told me of the man who never paid him after he worked for three days, he told me that he had no home, no family, and then he told me that he was so grateful. He looked at me and told me to always keep God in my heart, that God would lead me home. He told me how he was struck in the head with a club, and then he told me that God had placed a hand over his head, keeping that club from killing him. He said, "Thank you, God." I gave him seconds of salad, he gave me seconds of faith. This man came into my life in just seconds, and has changed me. He let me see a glimpse of God's light and pieces of God's magic.

I have friends who are angels, and angels who are friends. Life gave me them, and they give me life. I thank God for them everyday. Thank you, my angels, my friends.

Amy Westerman
Holy Cross High School
Louisville, Kentucky

Index by School

Saint Joseph Hill Academy
Staten Island, NY
Samantha Ecker   22

Saint Joseph's Academy
Baton Rouge, LA
Erica Balhoff   24

**Saint Maria Goretti
High School**
Philadelphia, PA
Kathy Grasso   20

Saint Scholastica Academy
Chicago, IL
Colleen J. Duffy   33

Saint Viator High School
Arlington Heights, IL
Joseph Emmons   99

Saint Vincent High School
Petaluma, CA
Bridget Venckus   112

Schools of the Sacred Heart
San Francisco, CA
Katheryn Patterson   104

Shanley High School
Fargo, ND
Jeff Markwardt   115

**Union Catholic Regional
High School**
Scotch Plains, NJ
Guy G. Werner III   35

**University of San Diego
High School**
San Diego, CA
Nate Scatena   19

**Ursuline Academy
of Cincinnati**
Cincinnati, OH
K. S. C.   95

**Villa Joseph Marie
High School**
Holland, PA
Christine Metzger   54

**Xaverian Brothers
High School**
Westwood, MA
Scott Gosselin   42

Xavier Preparatory School
New Orleans, LA
Irene Sola'nge McCalphin   118